Foreword I

The CHURCH *That* PRAYS TOGETHER

INSIDE THE *Prayer Life* OF 10 *Dynamic* CHURCHES

Elmer L. Towns & Daniel Henderson

NAVPRESS

For a free catalog
of NavPress books & Bible studies call
1-800-366-7788 (USA) or 1-800-839-4769 (Canada).

www.NavPress.com

The Navigators is an international Christian organization. Our mission is to advance the gospel of Jesus and His kingdom into the nations through spiritual generations of laborers living and discipling among the lost. We see a vital movement of the gospel, fueled by prevailing prayer, flowing freely through relational networks and out into the nations where workers for the kingdom are next door to everywhere.

NavPress is the publishing ministry of The Navigators. The mission of NavPress is to reach, disciple, and equip people to know Christ and make Him known by publishing life-related materials that are biblically rooted and culturally relevant. Our vision is to stimulate spiritual transformation through every product we publish.

ISBN-13: 978-1-60006-348-0
ISBN-10: 1-60006-348-9

Cover design by Marcy Shultz

Some of the anecdotal illustrations in this book are true to life and are included with the permission of the persons involved. All other illustrations are composites of real situations, and any resemblance to people living or dead is coincidental.

Unless otherwise identified, all Scripture quotations in this publication are taken from the HOLY BIBLE: NEW INTERNATIONAL VERSION® (NIV®). Copyright © 1973, 1978, 1984 by International Bible Society. Used by permission of Zondervan Publishing House. All rights reserved. Other Scripture quotations are taken from the *New King James Version* (NKJV). Copyright © 1982 by Thomas Nelson, Inc. Used by permission. All rights reserved; the *Holy Bible, New Living Translation* (NLT), copyright © 1996, 2004. Used by permission of Tyndale House Publishers, Inc., Carol Stream, Illinois 60188. All rights reserved.

Printed in the United States of America

1 2 3 4 5 6 7 8 / 12 11 10 09 08

Behind the headlines of every notable praying church you always find a faithful handful of unsung heroes who passionately seek the face of God and intercede for the needs of His people. In writing this book, we recognize that many of those names, unknown to us, will receive a profound and eternal reward someday for their diligent warfare on their knees. Praying churches are built by humble, praying people. They are the story behind the story.

Two such heroes of the faith who inspired both of us were R. C. Worley and Bill Sheehan. We dedicate this book to the memory of their lives of prayer and to countless others like them whom we will meet someday in heaven.

Elmer L. Towns and Daniel Henderson

FOREWORD

I love this book.

I love this book because it places prayer in the proper priority—Number 1—for growing, healthy churches. Too often modern church-growth books emphasize visitation evangelism, preaching evangelism, or TV evangelism. All of these methods are important, but none is as imperative as prayer. Without prayer, evangelism isn't possible.

When my husband, Bill Bright, won the Templeton Prize for Progress in Religion from the John Templeton Foundation in London, England, he was given approximately $1 million. He didn't take it for himself but rather invested it in prayer ministry through Campus Crusade for Christ to reach the world. For seven years, conferences on fasting and prayer were held across the United States. I praise God that many Christians learned how to get answers from God by aggressive fasting and prayer.

It was at a conference that I met Elmer Towns, who was one of the counselors with Bill in planning these conferences. Of course,

Dr. Towns has written dozens of books on prayer and has been used of the Lord to call multiplied thousands to a fresh experience of prayer and fasting though his work.

Daniel Henderson served as pastor for one of my dearest friends in this life, Winifred Verbica. She often has commented on the impact Daniel has had as a prayer-focused, local-church pastor. For over twenty-five years, Daniel has modeled prayer ministry in the church and has worked with pastors to raise prayer to a new level.

I love the format of this book. It doesn't look at just big churches or little churches; rather it looks at *praying* churches. In some of these chapters I feel as if I'm tiptoeing into a prayer meeting and listening to the people pour out their hearts to God. In other places I feel as if I'm looking over the shoulders of saints as they intercede. These chapters thrill my heart because they not only talk about prayer, but they also show what happens when God's people pray.

Let the examples in this book inspire you to a greater time in prayer. If you are a pastor, I think this book can transform your ministry—and also your women's ministry, youth ministry, Sunday school ministry, and every ministry of the church. My prayer is that God will use this book to change the prayer life of all churches.

Sincerely in Christ,

Vonette Bright

CONTENTS

ACKNOWLEDGMENTS

My personal thanks to Dr. Elmer L. Towns who, in past years, was my professor and mentor — and today is a colleague, friend, and coauthor. I am especially indebted to Pastor Jim Cymbala for the example of his enduring pastoral leadership and prayer passion. Thanks also to Dee Duke for his faithfulness and friendship. The women of Arcade Church are treasured intercessors and catalysts for renewal. I am grateful for my growing partnership with Paul Covert and Cal Jernigan at Central Christian Church in Mesa, Arizona. Finally, I praise God for the model of evangelistic passion I discovered in Pastor Khanh Quoc Huynh and his people at Vietnamese Baptist Church in Houston, Texas. Of course, I could not have done any of this work without the patient love and support of my wife, Rosemary, and the encouragement of Justin, Jordan, and Heather — my three Christ-loving children.

Daniel Henderson

Appreciation extended to Linda Elliott, Tricia Hicks, Kristin Wolfe, and Dan Marchant for their work on the manuscript. Also appreciation to my wife, Ruth, for fifty-five years of love and prayer support. Appreciation to the pastor and staff of Second Baptist Church in Houston, Texas; Thomas Road Baptist Church in Lynchburg, Virginia; Lakeview Wesleyan Church in Marion, Indiana; Christ Fellowship in Palm Gardens, Florida; and to the many churches contributing to chapter 10.

Elmer L. Towns

INTRODUCTION

We believe in prayer because Jesus said, "Men always ought to pray and not lose heart" (Luke 18:1 NKJV). Jesus commands us to pray and describes the length of time to do it: "Could you not watch with Me one hour?" (Matt. 26:40 NKJV). We both want to be passionately obedient to the commands of Jesus Christ. Therefore, we pray.

Neither of us claims to be a great hero of prayer, nor do we claim to get greater answers to prayer than anyone else. Probably the greatest prayer warriors in the United States are unknown believers who, by spending much time on their knees, accomplish much for the Lord. One reason for their success is the fact that they are unknown. They are humble, saying nothing about their prayer ministry and giving God all the glory.

While we may not be the greatest men of prayer living, we want to do everything we can to motivate the church to prayer. We write books on prayer, we hold seminars to teach people how to pray, and now we are writing this book, which we hope will accomplish the passion of our hearts. If, after you read it, you pray more, we've accomplished half of our passion. If you get your church to pray more, we've accomplished all of our passion.

This book presents what several praying churches across the country are doing and the prayer principle each one exemplifies. What's more, you'll see that you can apply these principles to your own church. We could have written about literally dozens and dozens of churches that are doing remarkable things in prayer, but we could pick only a handful. How did we ever select which ones to feature? First, we wanted to look at several different denominations, because people from different theological persuasions can pray and get answers to their prayers. Second, we wanted to look at different sizes of churches. We believe small-, medium-, and mega-size churches are all uniquely privileged by God to do His work through prayer.

Because we believe God can use old-fashioned churches that worship the same way they did when they were founded, we looked at them. But we also wanted to include some of the up-to-date modern-worship or organizational styles such as multi-site churches, attractional churches, and intentionally multicultural churches.

We wanted to include churches from across the country. Whereas we believe there is no such thing as a true "Southern" or "Western" church, we do believe sections of the country have specific characteristics. Why did we do this? So no one in any part of America could say, "They may pray like that in the South (or North or East or West), but prayer doesn't work like that where I live."

Also, notice we believe anyone can pray and touch the heart of God: children, youth, adults, rich, poor, and any ethnic group. Anyone and everyone can pray. Too often people think of a prayer warrior as an old widow who spends most of her life on her knees in intercession for the work of her church. While we praise God for every elderly woman who prays, we know there are terrific young intercessors who put aside the pursuit of rock music, the vanities of video games, and the addictiveness of physical sports to give themselves to prayer. And don't forget high schoolers; the greatest prayer meeting in the United States is held each October by high schoolers who "Meet You at the Pole." Since 1991, See You at the Pole has grown to God-sized proportions.

As you read, watch for the many different ways to pray. If you see a prayer term you're unfamiliar with, check the appendix starting on page 133 for its definition. Also, you'll read about many answers to prayer. Some answers are small; that's fine. We believe in praying for minutia. But some answers are astounding miracles where God clearly intervened to bring about a great revival in the church, a great harvest of souls, or a great amount of money supplied to His work. Don't let these large events overwhelm you. Instead ask, "What could I learn from this work of God?" and "How can I take my next step of faith to trust God for more?"

I (Daniel) was a student of Elmer Towns, and as a result of his teaching, I was on a twenty-one-day fast while a student at Liberty University. It was because of that fast that I met my wife, Rosemary. It's reassuring to know that your choice of a lifemate came out of a concentrated prayer and fasting before God!

I (Elmer) was on a forty-day fast when a publisher asked me, "What great answer did you get by fasting?" I frankly told him, "I'm not fasting to get anything from God; I'm fasting to know God." The publisher was so impressed that he said, "Write me a book on knowing God." That evening I went to my room and began the book that I called *God Encounters,* the story of thirteen people in Scripture who experienced the atmospheric presence of God. That experience changed their lives; it also changed mine.

Now we want to challenge you to a deeper life of prayer. Therefore, before you begin reading, we ask that you would first bow your head and dedicate yourself to read the entire book. Second, ask the Holy

Spirit to guide you to understand more about prayer, more than you've ever understood before. Third, ask God what you must do as a result of reading this book. When you come to the end, make a fourth commitment — to pray as He has taught you from this book.

May God use this book to make you and your church greater intercessors for God.

Written from our homes at the foot of the Blue Ridge Mountains,
Elmer L. Towns and Daniel Henderson

SHARE YOUR STORY

As you read this book, you will be inspired by the stories of congregations that have forged a significant prayer culture. You also may be inspired to share how your church has experienced a movement of prayer. To share your story, go to www.strategicrenewal.com, click on "Share Your Prayer Story," and tell us about it.

CHAPTER 1

A PASTOR OF PRAYER

Jefferson Baptist Church
Jefferson, Oregon

In the fall of 1988, Pastor Dee Duke received a letter from Dr. Joe Aldrich, president of Multnomah School of the Bible in Portland, Oregon. It invited Salem-area pastors to a four-day get-together at the coast for a first-ever Prayer Summit. This unusual event would encompass prayer with no agenda, no programs, and no speakers.

At the time, Pastor Duke wasn't excited about the prospect of praying for four days. It sounded boring. Reluctantly, however, he decided to attend, but his plan was to skip the prayertimes. He would walk on the beach, think about his life, write a letter of resignation to his church, and try to figure out what to do next.

His decision to respond to that invitation led to a radical renewal in his life that forever changed the essence and trajectory of his pastoral ministry. Today, he is recognized as a humble, insightful, and very effective pastor whose model of prayer inspires church leaders around the world.

GOD'S CALL

Jefferson Baptist Church began as a church plant in 1973 in Jefferson, Oregon, a small farming community in the Willamette Valley. Pastor Duke and his wife assisted the founding pastor while attending Western Bible College. After graduation in 1975, they returned to the dairy farm owned by Pastor Duke's father in Washington State in hope of fulfilling the young man's high school dream to be the world's greatest dairy farmer. Even though he had finished Bible college, Pastor Duke's real love was the farm.

In 1976 his dreams were interrupted by a call from the leaders at Jefferson Baptist: "We don't know if you've heard, but things haven't gone well here. The pastor left, and we're down to just a few people. We're planning to close the church, but we thought that before we did, we would call you. If you and your wife will come back to Jefferson, we'll keep the church open and try to make a go of it."

Although plans were in place for Pastor Duke to take over the farm, he had a longing to use his ministry training. His father advised, "If you don't give this a try, you'll always regret it." So the pastor and his family packed up and moved to Jefferson. Reflecting on that decision, he says, "I was an extreme introvert. I struggled with relationships, and the whole thought of being a pastor scared me to death. But I couldn't shake the strong sense that God was calling me back to be the pastor."

About twenty-five people attended the church when Pastor Duke arrived. In spite of his lack of experience, God blessed the congregation with more people, and the church steadily grew. They met in the local grade school gym until the fall of 1979 when they moved into their own building on five acres of land. By 1980, Jefferson Baptist had almost two-hundred people.

But the setbacks during those eight years took a toll. The church was full of disunity and financial problems. Many people left, and the ones who stayed weren't happy. Pastor Duke says, "I tried as hard as I knew how to be a good pastor and to do the things that would cause our church to grow. My father used to say that there wasn't anything I couldn't accomplish if I was willing to work hard enough. So every time someone left the church, I would work a little harder, put in more time, start another program. But nothing seemed to work. I seemed to upset and offend people no matter what I did and no matter how hard I tried."

READY TO QUIT, RELUCTANT TO PRAY

By the end of 1988, Pastor Duke felt bitter and angry at God — and at most of the people in the church. After obediently giving up his dream of farming to serve the church, he felt God's blessing had eluded him. He became disillusioned, weary, and depressed, concluding that God had not really called him to ministry after all. By then the dairy was sold, and he had no idea what he was going to do with his life. He just knew that he was going to resign from Jefferson Baptist Church and start his life over.

That is when he reluctantly decided to attend the Prayer Summit.

Pastor Duke went to the first session just to be polite. After just twenty minutes into prayer, it occurred to him that he had tried everything over the years *except* prayer. His prayer life was shallow, and church prayertimes were sparsely attended. But God arrested his attention and gripped his heart early in that Prayer Summit and changed him in those four days.

"For the next four days God turned me inside out," he recalls.

"He convicted me of my prayerlessness, my independent spirit, and my belief that I could accomplish this 'pastor thing' with enough work. I had never realized how arrogant I was. I knew things had to change."

Pastor Duke didn't miss a single session at the summit and hasn't missed a step since then in his desire to be a praying pastor who leads a praying church.

A CHANGED PASTOR, CHURCH, AND COMMUNITY

Following the summit, Pastor Duke became convinced that his church needed to make prayer the central focus of its ministry. He started by confessing his prayerlessness to his congregation and publicly pledging to be a man dedicated to prayer. He also set seven specific goals for his life and ministry:

1. Spend one uninterrupted hour per day praying by himself.
2. Spend one hour per day praying with at least one other person.
3. Pray for everyone in the church by name weekly.
4. Pray at least once per month with other pastors.
5. Preach on prayer for three months.
6. Plan four major church prayer events each year (always to precede a major evangelistic thrust).
7. Identify the church's "farm" (twenty miles in every direction from the church), claim it, and target prayer for it.

He opened the church from 9-10 p.m. for prayer and continues to do so to this day. Pastor Duke also began to devote a major part of his mornings to intercessory prayer for individuals and families in the church. Besides praying for their needs, he asked God to motivate his people to pray. He took his charge from John 17:9, in which Jesus prays to the Father: "I pray for them. I am not praying for the world, but for those you have given me, for they are yours." Pastor Duke's example of prayer, intercession for his people, and relentless obedience to the call to pray has brought great blessing to his life, church, and community.

In Jefferson, with a population of 2,200, the church has grown to an average attendance of 1,400 people in four weekend services. Pastor Duke says, "The more we prayed, the more God put His heart in us to reach the lost. We experienced a growing sense of urgency to reach our neighbors and the world. We grew in boldness and in creative ways to reach out to the lost. Almost everybody in the church began praying for lost friends, work associates, family members, mission efforts, and countries around the world."

Jefferson Baptist has planted three daughter congregations in Albany, Turner, and Corvallis. The pastors of these new congregations were trained at Jefferson Baptist and continue to carry the DNA of prayer and outreach with Christ-honoring results. The mother church has raised funds to help support each pastor and assist the new churches in buying property.

SCHOOL OF HARD KNOCKS

Pastor Duke admits that he hasn't "arrived," nor has he implemented his passion perfectly. He advises other pastors not to become too pushy in their enthusiasm for prayer. "In our eagerness we want to pressure everyone to participate. But many in our churches are immature and reluctant," he explains.

He has learned the wisdom of giving people progressive opportunities to grow in prayer as the Spirit stirs their hearts. He encourages everyone to come to at least one prayertime a month. Some might become interested in prayer through periodic prayerwalks in the community or even in another country. He also tries to offer periodic prayer events that motivate everyone.

Eventually, people commit to attending prayertimes weekly or to praying regularly for those who do not know Christ. A visit to Jefferson Baptist's very unassuming Web site (www.jeffersonbaptistchurch.org) will tell you that the congregation has really caught the vision as they have some forty prayertimes a week. Many prayer ministries have developed, including targeted prayer teams and an official "church intercessors" group (committed to one-hundred hours of prayer for the year, fifty at home and fifty at church). Pastor Duke assures pastors that, in time, the vision will take root and the commitment will follow.

A second major mistake he cautions against is to allow prayer experiences to grow beyond the necessary effort to train skilled leaders. Pastor Duke regrets the prayer meetings people in his church have attended that weren't led by someone who modeled prayer and understood the key principles of effective prayer. To overcome that mistake, he regularly conducts a leadership class that includes a variety of important topics, one of the most essential being prayer.

WISDOM FOR WILLING PASTORS

For those pastors willing to turn from a prayerless ministry to embrace a vision for heartfelt change, Pastor Duke willingly offers advice from his own journey. In fact, every January Jefferson Baptist hosts a conference for pastors that attract leaders from many states and several countries. He speaks of his pathway to a praying life, the principles he's learned about the incalculable blessings of prayer in the church, and the practical principles for implementing prayer. Some of his salient points are:

Believe that prayer is essential.

Almost everyone believes that prayer is important. But there is a difference between believing that prayer is important and believing it is essential. "Essential" means there are things that will not happen without prayer. He says, "There are many contributing factors to successful ministry, especially in the area of winning the lost. Prayer alone may not get results. But without prayer, even the best program, discipline, or plan will be frustrated and fail. Those who believe that prayer is essential—not just important—will have a passion and fervency that will persuade others to join them." He shares that the stronger his belief that prayer is absolutely essential, the stronger his zeal and passion have become. He believes zeal and passion are the keys to good leadership when motivating a congregation to pray for the lost.

Model your belief.

Pastor Duke knows the first step in motivating a congregation to make prayer essential is to model this belief. He believes that a prayer commitment is much like budgeting money: You write down your goals, and then consistently allocate your time according to those goals. Not only does he do this through preaching, participating in prayer gatherings, and interceding for his flock—but also through praying with other pastors.

Every week, he and the pastors around the Jefferson area gather for four hours of prayer and sharing. They bear burdens, engage in honest accountability, and pray for each other and the surrounding community. This sacrificial, unselfish prayer commitment speaks volumes to the congregation.

Target the men.

Pastor Duke has learned that getting the hearts of the men, who are often the hardest to reach, you get the hearts of the wives and families. He regularly calls the men to a high and holy commitment of accountability and believes this has been a vital part of the church's health. He asks the men to join a regular accountability group. Within that group each man commits to:

- A regular Bible-reading plan
- Praying for the needs of the church, using a regular update letter that Pastor Duke sends
- Praying with his wife two times a week
- Reading twenty pages in a book every week
- Responding openly and consistently to the needs of other men in his group
- Being consistently involved in corporate prayer at least two times a month

As these groups have gathered, the spiritual life of each man has deepened. Marriages have improved and the spiritual level of the church has risen to new levels.

Provide many opportunities to pray.

Bite-sized opportunities to pray are very important. Often Pastor Duke begins by asking people to engage in a one-time commitment to pray for fifteen minutes for five days. He believes anyone can do this. As they begin, he asks the Holy Spirit to capture their hearts with a growing love for Jesus and His presence.

Pastor Duke believes it's best if those opportunities are designed so the congregation can see answers. It's certainly important to pray for unsaved relatives who live halfway across the country. But something happens to a congregation when people see a person they've been praying for accept Christ as Savior, become a growing believer, and get involved in a church.

At Jefferson Baptist, he encourages people to pray for neighbors, local friends, and coworkers. The church plans four major prayer events a year, each followed by an evangelistic event. For example, every year before Easter, regular attendees put the names of ten local people who don't go to church on a prayer card. They commit to pray for them every day and invite them to church on Easter Sunday. They turn in the cards and put them in a big bowl. Starting ten days before Easter, the congregation engages in around-the-clock prayer for the people on the cards. The day before Easter, they commit to twenty-four hours of fasting. Each time a person is prayed for, the pray-er marks the card and puts it back in the bowl. By Easter morning, each person has been prayed for numerous times.

The pastor says, "The first year we did this we had over five hundred in attendance on Easter morning—over fifty responded to an invitation to accept Christ as their Savior!"

Another prayer initiative he started was to involve intercessors in a community prayer effort. They record the name of every person who lives within a twenty-minute drive of the church. Four times a year the intercessors send a card to them, asking for prayer-requests. "We want our community to know we are a praying church. When they have needs, they'll know where to go," he says.

Jefferson Baptist high school students prayerwalk for the unsaved. Each morning a group of young people prayerwalks around the school's track. Besides getting exercise, they pray for teachers and students by name. This has been extremely effective and been the impetus for the launching of a Saturday-night service geared toward youth. Many of prayerwalkers come to the service to meet the young people they've been praying for.

Don't give up!

Pastor Duke offers this encouragement: "If you want to see your church develop a passion for prayer and for the lost, don't give up! It may take awhile to get your congregation motivated and on board. Start slow and keep trying. Make them aware that the leaders of the church are praying, and put in front of them opportunities to pray."

Expect blessings.

Pastor Duke and the people of Jefferson Baptist have identified twenty-one blessings that God has brought into the church since they devoted their lives to the ministry of prayer. Some of these tangible blessings include a marked increase in unity, a deeper and evident love for one another, and a growing vision for evangelism and missions.

One blessing is especially important to him personally. "God has changed me. I had always loved God deeply, and I went into ministry to obey Him. But I had just tolerated people. I had few relational skills and little desire to develop close relationships. For me, 'loving people' had been pure duty. But when the people of Jefferson Baptist began to pray for me, God dramatically changed my heart toward the people — and He has changed their hearts toward me as well."

Out of this growing movement of prayer, Jefferson Baptist's mission statement was born. "Jefferson Baptist Church is the 'I love You' church," Pastor Duke declares. "We are continually saying, 'I love You' to God, to each other, to the greater body of Christ, to our unsaved neighbors and friends, and to the whole world, until the whole world can say, 'I love You, God.'"

The church motto has become "Much prayer, much blessing; little prayer, little blessing; no prayer, no blessing." Under Dee Duke's prayerful leadership, church members are asking God to bless them so they can be a blessing to the world. "Thanks to all those sheep who pray faithfully for me," he says. "I now love shepherding even more than I loved taking care of the cows on the old family farm!"

CHAPTER 2

THE WEEKLY CHURCHWIDE PRAYER MEETING

The Brooklyn Tabernacle
Brooklyn, New York

It was 6:15 p.m. on a Tuesday evening. What a day it had been! At 6:00 a.m., 180 people boarded a chartered flight in Minneapolis bound for New York City. After arriving, we filed into the subway and emerged right in front of the Brooklyn Tabernacle. We enjoyed a delicious lunch, a couple hours of sharing with Pastor Jim Cymbala and his staff, a quick dinner on the streets of Brooklyn, and an early entrance into the Tuesday-evening prayer meeting at the recently remodeled facility on Smith Street.

The churchwide prayer meeting was scheduled to begin at 7:00 p.m. as it did every Tuesday. By 5:45 p.m. it was hard to find a seat on the main floor because so many people had come early and eagerly to pray. The auditorium soon filled to capacity with more than 4,000 hungry hearts.

I (Daniel) was thrilled that more than fifty pastors from ten states had joined us for this powerful exposure to the heart and practice of a praying church. This was my eighth trip to the Tuesday-night prayer meeting, and it was the second time I brought a chartered plane full of friends. But at 6:15 p.m., it was no longer about the excitement of the trip or the thrill of exposing friends to this prayer experience. It was about me. I felt compelled to go to the front, kneel at the altar, and give my burdens to the Lord. I was facing some major decisions and carrying heavy responsibilities. I needed a touch from the Lord. Before the night was over, I received an answer to my prayers. Somehow, I think 4,000 others did as well.

INADEQUATE BUT WILLING

Anyone who has read Pastor Jim Cymbala's book *Fresh Wind, Fresh Fire* remembers his story well. In 1971, when he and his wife, Carol, took over the leadership of the humble handful of believers called the Brooklyn Tabernacle, they felt inadequate but hungry for God's grace. Their hearts haven't changed, but the Lord's response to their cry has yielded profound fruit in Brooklyn and all around the world.

The Brooklyn Tabernacle Web site (www.brooklyntabernacle.org) catches the essence of this ministry so well when it states that the Cymbalas "have replaced education with steadfast prayer, dependence on the power of the Holy Spirit, and complete reliance on God's mercy. The resulting ministry of the Brooklyn Tabernacle has been blessed by steady growth in numbers and spiritual fervor." This 10,000-member congregation is far beyond what the Cymbalas could have imagined when they arrived to serve fifteen people in a dilapidated building on Atlantic Avenue. Their first Sunday offering was $85, and their first year's salary was $3,800.

SEVEN PRINCIPLES FROM BROOKLYN

I have enjoyed the privilege of a friendship with Pastor Cymbala. I have heard him speak dozens of times in person and countless times on recordings. He has spoken in my church; I have preached in his Sunday services. Of course, I have remained a strong advocate of the Tuesday-evening prayertime. I have been immeasurably blessed by Pastor Cymbala's teaching and example and learned seven principles that stand out in this amazing prayer movement in Brooklyn.

1. Attractive weakness

At the heart of the Tuesday-evening prayer meeting is the realization of man's utter weakness before God and in handling the issues of life. The genesis of the prayer meeting was Jim and Carol's deep sense of inadequacy in light of the challenges of ministry during those early days.

Pastor Cymbala often tells the story of one Sunday evening in his first year at Brooklyn when he was exhausted, discouraged, and empty. He was working a second job, trying to lead a church without the normal formal education, and feeling incapable of handling the many demands of broken people in the hard mission field of inner city New York. A few minutes into his sermon he stopped, called the church to prayer, put his face in his hands as he stood at the pulpit, and began to weep.

In the moments to follow, God worked powerfully in the church, including the open repentance of an usher who had been taking money from the offerings. This was an early glimpse of God's power to accomplish more in a few minutes of earnest prayer than is often achieved in years of human striving.

Over and over, God has impressed the people of the Brooklyn Tabernacle with the truth that humble, honest, and desperate cries before God invite His power to move. These early lessons allowed Pastor Cymbala to delight in his weaknesses (see 2 Cor. 12:9–10), knowing that God could use him just as he is as long as he and his people would seek the Lord first.

In those early days, he would never have believed that he would become the pastor of a large church and a best-selling author, or that his wife would direct a Grammy award–winning choir. To this day, the Cymbalas seem less impressed with these achievements than anyone as they continue to cultivate the determination and delight of staying weak before God.

2. Holy discontent

God has given Pastor Cymbala a holy discontent with status-quo ministry that outwardly appears to be successful but lacks the authenticity of "fresh wind and fresh fire." He often declares that he would rather die than simply go through the motions of socially acceptable and comfortable ministry routines.

During the first couple years of his ministry, Pastor Cymbala developed a chronic cough. Noting his exhaustion, his in-laws paid for him to spend some time in Florida to rest and recuperate. While on a chartered deep-sea fishing trip, he experienced a moment with God that changed his life. As he sat at the back of the boat contemplating the complexities and burdens of pastoral ministry, he began to cry out in desperation for a fresh touch from God.

As he recounts it, the Lord spoke to him clearly. "If you and your wife will lead My people to pray and call upon My name, you will never lack for something fresh to preach. I will supply all the money that's needed, both for the church and for your family, and you will never have a building large enough to contain the crowds I will send in response."[1]

The pastor returned to the Brooklyn Tabernacle to declare that from that time on the prayer meetings would be the barometer of everything they would do at the church. The Tuesday-night prayer service became the gauge by which they would judge the success or failure of their ministry. Jim and Carol Cymbala had concluded that this was the measure by which God would bless the church.

Pastor Cymbala, quoting the words of a visiting preacher, often notes, "You can tell how popular a church is by who attends on Sunday morning. You can tell how popular the preacher is by who attends on Sunday night. You can tell how popular Jesus is by who attends the prayer meeting." He seems discontent with anything but the supreme popularity of Jesus as He is honored through humble, God-dependent people and ministry.

3. Vertically focused prayer

Genuine, passionate worship permeates the culture of the Brooklyn Tabernacle. Carol Cymbala's ministry in music and the influence of the Brooklyn Tabernacle Choir is well recognized. Of course, this love for music with heartfelt lyrics and soulful tunes has been essential since the beginning.

This same longing for real worship marks all of the praying at the church. One of the most surprising aspects of the Tuesday-evening prayer meetings for first-time visitors is the very dim lighting in the auditorium. This design is to keep participants from being distracted with the "horizontal"—looking around at others and becoming interested with the surroundings. The intent is to encourage individuals to quietly worship the Lord.

The entire prayer meeting is punctuated with spontaneous worship through song, usually lead by Pastor Cymbala and a small team of singers. Most of the instrumentalists at the Brooklyn Tabernacle play by ear, which gives him the freedom to sing melodies that might be on his heart at any given moment. The first fifteen to twenty minutes (sometimes more) of the prayer service are given to free-flowing worship through song and spoken praise.

Pastor Cymbala describes this longing for and delight in God's presence as a vital part of the heart of the church and evidence of the work of the Spirit. Often he asks, "If we do not delight on God's presence and nearness here on earth, why would we want to go to heaven where He is the centerpiece of everything?"

4. Holy Spirit reliance and responsiveness

Pastor Cymbala notes that the Holy Spirit is the spirit of prayer. He believes that it is the work and fullness of the Holy Spirit in one's life (and in a church) that produces a spirit of prayer.

One evening he and I (Daniel) sat in my office enjoying dinner between sessions at a conference. I shared with him my frustrations in motivating people to pray, a concern he hears often from pastors. I will never forget his words: "Daniel, you can't 'ought' people to pray. The Holy Spirit must draw them and move them to prayer. Don't ask your people to pray. Ask the Holy Spirit to work in them to give them the desire and determination to pray."

This adjustment of focus is a powerful one. Of course, it is indicative of his intimate sensitivity to and reliance on the Holy Spirit in all of life and ministry. Pastor Cymbala views the prayer meetings as a "Holy Ghost Emergency Room," where the Spirit of God meets people at their point of need in the context of crying out to God. The Spirit is always sufficient for their hurts, longings, disappointments, and hopes.

This reliance on the Holy Spirit is also seen in how he leads church services. The Tuesday-night prayer meeting is largely unscripted.

I have been in Tuesday-evening prayer meetings where the entire choir sang, where the pastors were up front to pray with people, where all the men were called forward to pray prior to the start, and even where Pastor Cymbala conducted a wedding. But knowing or not knowing these elements in advance in no way diminishes a keen sensitivity to the prompting of the Holy Spirit as the meeting progresses.

Sunday services are similar. The congregation knows there will be a sermon, an offering, a choir special, and some worship. However, the coordination of these elements is less a function of a written program (which they don't have) and more a function of being sensitive to the moment as the Holy Spirit directs. Again, this seems a small variation, but it does make a big difference and is based in a conviction about relying on and responding to the Holy Spirit.

Demonstrating a wonderful balance in his understanding of the Holy Spirit, Pastor Cymbala often observes that churches can become either an "insane asylum or a cemetery" in their practical understanding of the Holy Spirit. He is openly critical of those ministries that turn the work of the Spirit into a slick circus environment of spectacularism. He is equally concerned about those believers who seldom mention or emphasize the essential ministry and work of the Holy Spirit.

5. Aversion to novelty

Pastor Cymbala says it often and passionately: "We are not a model." Over the years, he has grown discontent with the common pursuit of novel models of church growth. He has an aversion to "numbers-oriented ministry," noting that the Bible seldom comments on the size of churches but instead emphasizes the spiritual health. He is openly critical of churches that believe in any sense that money, organization, cleverness, technology, leadership technique, or education is the secret to successful ministry. As the Brooklyn Tabernacle has become more "successful" in the eyes of observers, Pastor Cymbala has become less interested in anyone trying to duplicate what has happened there.

These concerns are based in his firm conviction that Jesus wants His house to be a house of prayer (Mark 11:15–18) — not preaching, programming, or entertaining formulas. The essence of the culture of the Brooklyn Tabernacle is a determination to seek the Lord at all times in collective prayer for direction and empowerment. The idea of imitating other ministries in order to be more "successful" is completely foreign. Pastor Cymbala and his congregation have learned that God can do more in ten minutes of heartfelt prayer than man can do in years of trying to be novel. This conviction continues to fuel their prayer efforts.

Another expression of prayer as the core of their reliance on God is the Prayer Band. Organized years ago by Pastor Kenneth Ware, a senior statesman on the church staff, it started as a series of all-night prayer meetings. The Prayer Band now has been structured to allow people to pray in three-hour shifts, seven days a week, twenty-four hours a day. They receive requests from church members and people all around the world. One of their primary emphases is to intercede during services, asking the Lord to work in His power and glory. This, too, is an expression of the congregation's disinterest in relying on human means for accomplishing a spiritual work. Pastor Cymbala recounts countless examples of Christ-honoring moments of ministry that have flowed from this determination to pray rather than parade new methodologies.

He further believes that God's power experienced in prayer is essential to Christians' influence in society. In one of the more profound statements in his first book, he writes,

Am I the only one who gets embarrassed when religious leaders in America talk about having prayer in public schools? We don't even have that much prayer in many churches! Out of humility, you would think we would keep quiet on that particular subject until we practice what we preach in our own congregations."[2]

He goes on to note that the early church changed their society not through human tactics but by virtue of their own experience of the spiritual power of Jesus Christ. They were people of humble reliance on God through the Word and prayer. And God did what only God could do through them in transforming lives within a pagan culture.

6. Fidelity to the Word

Early on, Pastor Cymbala recognized that his lack of formal theological education and his passion for prayer couldn't become an excuse for scriptural shallowness. He is an avid student of God's Word, maintaining a hungry heart and humble spirit as it relates to his pursuit of biblical learning.

Recognizing his need to consistently and accurately teach the word, he has connected weekly for many years with noted Bible teacher and pastor Warren Wiersbe. Beyond his personal commitment to study the text, this relationship has given Pastor Cymbala a much-desired accountability and collaboration in the Word. Even though he has a Pentecostal background, he has recognized his need for the mentoring of the older Wiersbe, a noted conservative evangelical scholar.

Pastor Cymbala firmly believes that the Bible is enough and that he has no latitude to go beyond "what is written" (1 Cor. 4:6).

He often reiterates the adage "If it's new, it isn't true, and if it's true, it isn't new." He writes, "The things of God have a circumference. They are preserved in a written body of truth. It is like a well—and no one has ever fathomed the depth of God's truth."[3]

On the other hand, he speaks often of his concern over sound doctrine without spiritual power. He grieves over academic rigor and theological bickering that doesn't lead people to be more like and more in love with Christ. Quoting the great puritan theologian William Law, Pastor Cymbala expresses his heart on this subject: "Read whatever chapter or Scripture you will, and be ever so delighted with it—yet it will leave you as poor, as empty and unchanged as it found you unless it has turned you wholly and solely to the Sprit of God, and brought you into full union with and dependence upon Him."[4]

This love for God's Word has been the authority and parameter for the ministry of the Brooklyn Tabernacle over the decades. As much as the church is noted for its prayer ministry, that ministry has been blessed and sustained because of Cymbala's determination to keep the honor and authority of God's Word at the center of all that occurs.

7. Accountability to Christ

Pastor Cymbala's constant and keen awareness of the ultimate evaluation of our lives and ministries before the penetrating eyes and final examination of Jesus Christ is critical. He often reflects on the fact that he does not want to arrive in eternity describing all he has done for Jesus in his life. He simply wants to fall on his face, thanking the Lord for what He has done through dependent and prayerful lives.

First Corinthians 3:12–13 (NKJV) says our "work will be shown for what it is, because the Day will bring it to light. It will be revealed with fire, and the fire will test the quality of each man's work." This separation of "gold, silver, and precious stones" from the common "wood, hay, and stubble" is a theme that clearly sustains the heart of prayer at the Brooklyn Tabernacle. Pastor Cymbala affirms that the Lord will not evaluate the quantity of what we have done, but the quality of our lives. It is not just what we have done but *why* and *for whom*. Perhaps this defines as well as anything else the passion behind the praying life of Jim Cymbala and his congregation.

In *Fresh Wind, Fresh Fire,* he probably expresses his heart for prayer in his church as clearly as ever:

> During countless Tuesday night prayer meetings I find myself encircled by the sacred sound of prayer and the intercession filling the church, spilling in to the vestibules, and overflowing from every heart present. As the meeting edges to a close, I overhear mothers petitioning for wayward children . . . men asking God to please help them find employment . . . others giving thanks for recent answers to prayer . . . tearful voices here and there. I can't help think, *this is closest to heaven as I will ever get in this life. I don't want to leave here. If I were ever invited to the White House to meet some dignitary, it would never bring the kind of peace and deep joy I sense here in the presence of people, calling on the Lord.*[5]

"The sacred sound of prayer." That is the sound that delights the heart of God, mystifies the angels, and thrills the heart of a real pastor. Jim Cymbala is such a pastor who will keep listening for that sound every week until he finally hears the praises beyond the gates of heaven.

CHAPTER 3

A TOTAL PROGRAM OF PRAYER

Second Baptist Church
Houston, Texas

Attendance at Second Baptist Church in Houston, Texas, began to explode exponentially after Dr. H. Edwin Young was called as pastor in 1978. Within nine years of Dr. Young's arrival, over 9,000 people attended church each Sunday. The monumental growth came because Pastor Young developed a strong prayer foundation in the church. He knew prayer was essential to building multiple programs and multiple evangelism outreaches.

Pastor Young led the congregation to build a new $34 million sanctuary with a double-decker balcony that seats 6,200 worshippers. The church was headed into the next century when it built recreation facilities and a fitness center so modern the Houston Rockets used its facilities. The campus also has outstanding IT facilities, a café, plus all the other needed church facilities.

Whereas some churches have a multitude of sports teams, Second Baptist has a multitude of leagues (a total of two dozen), including basketball for preschoolers right up to Senior Saints in its three gymnasiums. It also hosts multiple leagues on the church's five baseball, football, and soccer fields.

The church continued to grow, adding a west campus fifteen miles away on the I-10 corridor with a $38 million plant where 8,000 plus attend every Sunday. Then the church added a 35-acre north campus in 2004 with a 1,650-seat sanctuary that averages 5,000 every Sunday. The Pearland campus was added in 2005 as a video venue in a theatre with 450 in worship. Finally, the Cypress campus came about in the Berry Center with over 900 people coming.

The five campuses have a combined average of 24,500 people in weekly worship. "All of our outreach is an answer to prayer," says Executive Pastor John Barksdale.

Pastor Young felt that anything the church was called to do should have a spiritual director to see that it happened. The church added multiple age-graded coordinators for its Bible-teaching program, and then added musical directors for its many-pronged music program. The church has excelled in part because of these excellent directors. Pastor Young felt most churches leave their directors so busy that very little prayer is done. Other churches say prayer is everyone's job, but Pastor Young says, "Everyone's job is no one's job." So this aggressive pastor decided to do what most churches have not done: He appointed a full-time Director of Prayer, Dr. Jim DeLoach.

A COMPLETE PROGRAM

An executive staff member and a long-time friend of Pastor Young's, Pastor DeLoach laid the foundation for the prayer ministry as it is known today. Pastor Young says, "The continual expansive ministry of Second Baptist Church demands an extended foundation of prayer. Without prayer, we wouldn't have accomplished anything."

Pastor DeLoach organized a prayer program to involve more people in prayer than ever before. In addition to various prayer ministries, he began an annual prayer school and invited authorities on prayer to come to Houston to instruct intercessors in the art and practice of prayer. Then an annual prayer banquet was held to recognize faithful prayer warriors. Many attended not so much to hear the speaker but to hear of the great answers to prayer. Obviously these stories motivated everyone to greater prayer.

Second Baptist's comprehensive prayer program has many facets.

Online prayers

Second Baptist Church has brought its prayer ministry into twenty-first-century technology in several ways, including online prayers. The prayer-ministry staff maintains a computerized record of each prayer request. Requests pour into a central office from people in all five church locations throughout Houston, plus from around the world, and are compiled into a database.

Some people turn in prayer-requests via the Second Baptist Church Web site (www.second.org), which features an online prayer form for submitting urgent prayer-requests. These requests are reviewed by staff and then sent to the Prayer Room. As with every prayer-request, each submission is reviewed and any necessary pastoral action is taken.

Bible-study classes have a prayer coordinator who is responsible not only for leading prayer activities in class, but also for funneling these requests into the e-mail system where they are then circulated to all intercessors in the church. Each request is reviewed, and staffers take any necessary action, such as arranging a hospital visit. The e-mail is sent to the Prayer Room for prayer and onto the computer for prayer by computer intercessors.

Approved prayer intercessors have a log in and password to access these requests. They can pray whenever and wherever they are. And they are able to see when the request was last prayed for and how many times it has been prayed for.

Prayer-request cards and Prayergrams

Available in the church pews, these prayer-request cards are to be completed and placed in the offering plate or mailed to Second Baptist Church. A personally written "prayergram" is then sent to the person in need of prayer.

Prayergrams are handwritten cards sent by prayer-ministry intercessors to share God's love and concern for an individual's specific prayer need. This special group of volunteers picks up requests from the office weekly or has them mailed to them. They write prayergrams at home and return them via mail or in person. The prayer-ministry staff then proofreads each one before sending it to the recipient.

First Watch and Second Watch

The prayer ministry's frontline is called First Watch, Telephone Desk. In the Prayer Room, trained intercessors minister to hundreds of people who call the twenty-four-hour prayer line seeking intercession for many critical situations. Intercessors serve in the Prayer Room on the Woodway campus during a specific hour each week. Plans for Prayer Rooms at the other campuses are currently being developed.

Also in the Prayer Room is the church's First Watch, Silent Desk. Here, trained intercessors pray silently for prayer-requests for one hour each week.

In Second Watch, prayer warriors phone in from home each week to hear a detailed recorded message about needs for specific prayer situations. They commit to pray a specific hour each week for these special needs.

Prayer-office volunteers

Office volunteers are vital to the work of the church's prayer ministry. They handle multiple tasks such as answering the telephones, reviewing prayer cards, and assisting with clerical work. At Second Baptist Church, fifteen office volunteers coordinate updating the hospital list as well as all prayer-requests. They also do a follow-up phone call on prayer-requests to see how God has answered.

"We need to know results," says Danny Havard, Director of Pastoral Ministries. "We know that our intercessors are encouraged to greater faith when they hear what God has done. People pray better when they know what to pray for, and when they know their prayers make a difference, they intercede all the more."

Praying for the sick

The church has a ministry specifically organized for prayer hospital visitation. Pastors, specifically trained laypeople, and medical personnel who attend the church visit and pray with patients and their families.

In addition, certain Saturday-evening and Sunday-morning worship services are designated as healing services. The staff believes that "the prayer of faith will save the sick, and the Lord will raise them up" (James 5:15).

At these services, Dr. Young gives a message, then invites the people to go to one of seventeen stations on all three floors of the main auditorium. At each station are three people. The first person is a pastor whose task is to anoint the sick with oil (see James 5:14). The second person is a medical doctor who can give counsel. The third person is an intercessor whose task is to pray for the sick. The medical doctor gives professional insight in how to and for what the intercessor should pray. The healing service continues until everyone is ministered to.

Pastor Danny Havard says, "When people asked for prayer, they also asked for care." Many of those who came forward received some type of follow-up from church staff. Also a volunteer later phoned those who had requested prayer to see how prayer was being answered.

Prayer pagers

A prayer-pager program is currently in place that involves giving a pager to a church member or to his or her immediate family member with a serious level of need. The pager number is then distributed to friends, family, and church staff. When the number is dialed, a recorded message says, "You have reached the Second Baptist Church prayer pager for John Doe. At the tone please enter your five-digit zip code followed by the pound sign, and John will know you have prayed for him."

The pager is set on vibrate or a tone. When someone prays for "John," the pager goes off, and he can see where that pray-er lives. This is a tangible way for the person needing prayer to know someone has just prayed. The program began with three pagers and now averages fifteen to twenty being used at any given time.

Prayer Room

The church still recruits people into prayer watches. The term *watch* follows the admonition of Christ who asked, "Could you not watch with Me one hour?" (Matt. 26:40 NKJV).

Pastor Havard explains, "We offer a prayer ministry that fits into the busy schedule of modern-day Americans." All members are invited to pray one hour in the Prayer Room, which is open twenty-four hours a day; however, some come for several hours.

COMPREHENSIVE PRAYER

Dr. Young explained at the beginning of his ministry's prayer focus almost twenty-five years ago, "Everything that God wants the church to do, He expects individual believers to discipline themselves to do it, so we organize individuals to pray. We seek to be faithful in doing everything God wants the local church to do; we organize programs to accomplish the greatest good for the greatest number of people — all to the glory of God."

Second Baptist Church's prayer ministry is a total of many different types of intercession functioning on five different campuses. Each specific ministry track is customized to fit the specific prayer and care needs of church members, church prospects, or people around the globe. This results in having many prayer opportunities as people intercede on the people's behalf to God, praying for specific requests to be answered, and that God's perfect will would be done.

Executive Pastor John Barksdale says, "We as a body of believers are striving to be obedient to our calling to prayer. We believe prayer is a powerful and active tool God has given us to use in ministry for Him."

CHAPTER 4

WOMEN IN PRAYER

Arcade Church
Sacramento, California

This is the story of three women, a traditional church in transition, a new pastor, and a convergence in the presence of God that would launch a prayer movement among women. This movement would cross the nation and the world, and prove people in everyday circumstances have great potential to accomplish eternally significant work when they give God their undivided attention.

Alice Moss was a noted leader in her Sacramento-area African American church. She led worship on weekends, taught growing Bible studies among the women, and spearheaded successful women's retreats. In these contexts she experienced profound moments of "Scripture-fed, Spirit-led" prayer but couldn't seem to find that kind of experience outside the women's activities. In God's providence, she decided to visit Arcade Church in northeast Sacramento at around the same time the church called a new pastor. She didn't understand why the Lord would lead her to a larger, predominantly white, and very traditional congregation but knew in her heart that she was doing so in obedience to Him.

Collette McMurray had been a member of Arcade Church for decades. In 1992, Dr. Lee Toms retired as senior pastor after forty years of faithful and fruitful ministry. During the interim search for a new pastor, Collette began to feel a strange longing in her heart to worship more passionately. She began reading books on prayer and was discovering what it meant to pray the Word. Over the years she had traveled overseas on many missions projects where she saw people praying with passion. She notes, "God was working in marvelous ways in those countries. I felt His presence so powerfully. I wanted this to happen at my home church, but I didn't know how to get us there."

Dixie Weyel served as the children's director at Arcade. She was also a classically trained musician who sang often in services and helped in the music ministry. She always thought of worship as something that happened in conjunction with carefully planned agendas. During the months Arcade Church was searching for a new pastor, she also felt an unusual desire to discover how music and worship could become more vital in her prayer life. "Worship seemed like something we just tacked-on to the preaching in Sunday services. My prayers were all horizontal 'bless-me' prayers," she says. "In all of this, I was feeling a deep burden for a fresh discovery of worship."

In August 1993, God called me (Daniel) to pastor at Arcade. My passion was "worship-based prayer," basing all prayertimes in Scripture and praise rather than just on prayer-requests. This foundation of Scripture-fed, Spirit-led prayer brought people into the presence of God, which led to deep transformation and the sharing of authentic needs, rather than simply reviewing lists of requests. People noted the atmosphere was changing as I began to train other leaders in the disciplines of seeking God's face. I announced a first-ever Prayer Summit for the congregation to be held in January 1994, even though I'd never led a Prayer Summit and the church had never hosted one.

Nonetheless, three days were set aside at a nearby Christian camp where participants would gather for an unprecedented experience of the presence and person of Christ. Things were about to converge in a way that would forever change thousands of lives.

A MOMENT THAT LED TO A MOVEMENT

Alice, Collette, Dixie, about ninety others, and I arrived at Wolf Mountain Camp in the Sierra Nevada foothills on a Wednesday afternoon with high expectations, many reservations, and a willingness to try something new. From Wednesday evening until Saturday afternoon the group gathered in a large meeting room for spontaneous Scripture-reading, singing, and responsive prayers directed by me and a few minimally trained cofacilitators. The people also split into smaller gender-specific groups to continue the worship, which eventually led to a deep level of sharing their hearts and to interceding for one another. Two communion services highlighted the summit, we held several silent prayer seasons, and rich fellowship emerged around the meals.

As Alice describes it, "Not until that first summit was my heart truly satisfied in the Lord. So much of my corporate praying had been 'horizontal' and focused just on temporal needs. Those three days were 'vertical' as we sought God for who He is." Alice and her friend Deborah were the only African Americans at the summit and felt welcomed. "Even though we were like 'flies in the buttermilk,' we knew we had found the missing element our hearts had been longing for. The enemy tried to use race differences to keep me from going. God clearly called me to Arcade and kept me here for things that I could have never imagined."

Collette was selected to help facilitate a women's group at that summit. "I really had no idea what I was doing, even though the pastor had trained us as best he could," she remembers. "God knew my heart. He took my weakness and willingness and met me with His faithfulness. At this summit I realized why God had been preparing me with such a longing for worship and prayer." She fondly reflects on the healing work He did among the women when they sensed a nearness to Him, which enabled them to pray for each other more effectively. "Even though we had been in church together for years," Collette notes, "we had never experienced anything like this before."

Dixie went to the summit not knowing what to expect but feeling obligated to attend due to her staff position. It seemed strange that a group would just worship and pray for that long. But the divine stirrings in her heart were strong. She explains, "I fell in love with the Lord like never before as I experienced such a powerful outpouring of worship. I was especially amazed by the men as they engaged in something that was so fresh and real. We were all swept off our feet."

Little did these ladies imagine all God would do because of the spiritual spark that had ignited during those days. Alice would continue following the Lord's call to Arcade and eventually serve women's groups all around the United States by leading prayer experiences and teaching worship-based prayer. Collette and several other women would translate the momentum of that summit into weekly prayer experiences and a total of twenty-six subsequent summits at Arcade. And Dixie would eventually become director of women's ministries, igniting a fresh passion for Christ among the women of Arcade and beyond.

TWENTY-SIX SUMMITS AND COUNTING

The powerful stories of personal and corporate renewal begun at Arcade's first Prayer Summit and fuelled a passion in the hearts of many women to continue these times away for extraordinary prayer and worship. Men and women were trained to facilitate these gatherings, but the Holy Spirit was already motivating people to follow His leadership to experience even more.

Even though they really didn't know what they were doing, the church continued to sponsor these unusual three-day prayer experiences. Since 1994, the women of Arcade have held a summit every year and have participated in an additional churchwide summit annually. At the time it was a phenomenon, as no churches had hosted multiple prayer summits let alone held several every year. Now the movement is beginning to take off in other congregations. Arcade's example has inspired the vision of congregations across the nation.

James 5:16 (NKJV) says, "Confess your trespasses to one another, and pray for one another, that you may be healed. The effective, fervent prayer of a righteous man avails much." Through the principle of worship-based prayer, leading to the practice of James 5:16, marriages have been healed, women have been delivered from besetting sins, relationships have been reconciled, women have been called to ministry, and a powerful work of renewal is being sustained in the congregation.

In the spiritually passionate environment of prayer summits, the truth of God's Word has penetrated hearts. Women find a safe place to share. Authenticity and humility abound as they open their lives to one another and pray in faith for God's truth and Spirit to accomplish great things. It keeps happening, year after year.

Gloria's story is one of these transformation experiences. A Chinese immigrant, she was very shy and spoke only broken English. She had recently gone through a very painful divorce, and a variety of divorce-recovery ministries didn't seem to heal her deep pain. Yet, Gloria took the risk of attending a Prayer Summit. In that environment she opened her heart to the Spirit of Christ and to the women around her. Because of that amazing moment of being touched by the Lord, she began to come out of her shell with a new freedom. Today she regularly leads other women in prayer and serves as hospitality coordinator for a major Sunday school class at the church.

Then there is Lori, who attended her first summit while still a new Christian. Lori had not attended church before being saved, so she didn't know the worship songs and didn't understand much of the language being used. In fact, she didn't say a word for the three days of the summit. God was moving in her heart, however, and Lori kept attending the Arcade prayer summits and other prayer-focused gatherings, Today, ten years after her first summit, Lori leads the prayer ministry at her home church outside Sacramento and also works full time in a renewal ministry, organizing prayer events for churches across the nation.

Women have come by the scores from other churches to these three-day prayer experiences. Some have come from churches locked in deep division and strife. Others are pastors' wives. All have received more than they expected as they gave themselves unreservedly to the Lord in extended worship and allowed others to pray fervently for their needs. Alice Moss comments, "One pastor's wife came with deep pain. Even though she and her husband had attended and even led other summits in the past, she found something very special in this environment of just women. After the summit, her husband kept commenting about the change in her life as she experienced restored joy and intimacy with the Lord."

HEALING AND WHOLENESS

Since that weekend in January 1994, the women of Arcade have been meeting for worship-based prayer every Saturday morning. The prayer group is still going strong as Christ's presence and power meets them in practical ways.

"It has become a place where women can come to worship the Lord, knowing they can trust Him and one another with both the easy or very difficult issues of their lives," says Collette. The three women delight to tell story after story of the hearts, marriages, and homes that have been healed by God's grace in moments of intimate prayer. Women have been delivered from bondage to sin, bitterness toward their husbands, wounds from childhood, grief over difficult children, and fears about the future. Alice notes, "Women have literally come out of their shells of insecurity and introversion to become dynamic leaders in the prayer ministry as they have found a place to soak in the love of Christ and freely express their love for Him."

The Saturday-morning prayer gathering has attracted women from dozens of area churches as well. When God builds a fire, hearts come to share in the warmth. These women have found a place to trust the Lord for the struggles of their lives and churches. Many of these women are in leadership in other congregations — and the congregations are diverse. They come from Chinese-, Russian-, Japanese-, and Spanish-speaking churches.

BEYOND CHURCH WALLS

This movement of prayer has created a flood of interest far beyond Arcade Church. Out of the uniqueness of these extraordinary seasons of worship-based prayer, a conference emerged. The theme was "Imagine What God Could Do." Held at Arcade, the equipping event attracted five-hundred leaders from dozens of denominations and different states (and even several foreign countries) five years in a row. Of course, a central component was the opportunity for women to enjoy specialized tracks for training in prayer.

As the strategy has transitioned to a seminar focus, the Lord has opened many doors to take this movement to churches on the West Coast, across the country, and around the world. Requests have poured in for Alice Moss and others to teach women's groups, congregations, conference gatherings, and parachurch organizations in the principles of transformation emerging from worship-based prayer. To date, this prayer movement among the women of Arcade has been exported to churches in Canada, Kansas, Minnesota, and Texas through personal teaching. Of course, countless other churches have taken the vision and fire back to their congregations after conferences.

As this story of prayer has traveled, Alice and others from Arcade have led summits for mission agencies, pastors and their wives, and nationally renowned renewal ministries in several Midwestern states. Alice has shared her story and taught the principles at two national women's conferences hosted by Nancy DeMoss and her ministry, *Revive Our Hearts!* The women of Arcade have also enthusiastically shared with and equipped women in India, Romania, Brazil, Mexico, France, Indonesia, and China.

WOMEN MOBILIZING CREATIVE PRAYER

Back on the homefront, the women of Arcade continue to experience a growing passion to seek the face of God. Several times a year they sponsor an extended prayer day called "Times of Refreshing." Using the same Scripture-based, spontaneous format, they meet for an entire Saturday morning dedicated to prayer. As usual, women from around the community attend. Now the men desire to join in as stories of transformation continue to spread.

The women enjoy an annual event called "Women in White." Attendees wear white clothing with their focus on celebrating Christ as their bridegroom. Various themes are integrated into the evenings, using biblical teaching and focused prayer. Visual aids such as a throne, crown, candles, and colorful streamers enhance the experience.

Acting on their passion to reach out to women who don't typically connect with the church on Sunday mornings, the ladies of Arcade Church have now started a "Women of the Word" class for women with unsaved spouses, singles, or those whose husbands can't participate with them in a regular class. In addition to the sound teaching, the class is distinguished by significant doses of worship-oriented prayer.

Since that first summit, the women have been actively involved in the leadership of a weekly churchwide "Fresh Encounter" prayer service that has attracted groups numbering from twenty-five to five hundred. They have committed to a World Prayer Center at the church, Powerhouse Prayer (intercession during the services), and leading children in the Prayer Summit experience during Sunday school classes. The historic women's retreat also has taken on a new dimension as each getaway incorporates a strong worship-based prayer component. Women regularly speak of using worship-based prayer in their counseling with one another as a powerful way to experience heart transformation along with practical biblical application.

Perhaps most significantly, individual prayer experiences have been changed. As Dixie Weyel comments, "My own prayer life has been transformed as I have applied the approach and principles I've learned to my devotional reading and prayer experience. I will never be the same."

UNDIVIDED ATTENTION, UNANTICIPATED IMPACT

One of the common slogans around Arcade Church is "God is always glad to oblige when you give Him your undivided attention." The story of the Arcade women is simply an example of what God can do when we regularly take time to seek His face, days (not just minutes) at a time.

Arcade has gone through numerous challenging transitions. I (Daniel) was eventually called away after eleven fruitful years and now lead a full-time national effort in prayer and renewal. The next pastor to come to Arcade died from surgery complications after serving the church for only a few months. But today a dynamic young pastor who grew up at Arcade is leading the church into new forms of ministry targeting a younger generation.

And the women still pray. They inspire others with their stories, experiences, and biblical teachings. When asked if they will stop having those extended summits, Saturday gatherings, and fresh experiences of prayer, their response was clear: "Not in our lifetime. We've been told by our pastor and God's Word to carefully guard what has been given to us. So we are going to stand guard, keep praying, and keep reproducing this vision in younger women. It's all just so remarkable."

CHAPTER 5

THE PRAYER ROOM

Lakeview Wesleyan Church
Marion, Indiana

The concept of a prayer room may have begun in the Metropolitan Baptist Church of London, England, in 1830. In the church basement, directly under the pulpit, stood a parlor table surrounded by chairs with small, round spindle legs and red pillows. Whenever Charles Spurgeon preached, a special group of "watchers" knelt in prayer on the red pillows. These people were called "watchers" after the exhortation by Jesus in the garden of Gethsemane when He begged, "Could you not watch with Me one hour?" (Matt. 26:40 NKJV). This group prayed for spiritual power on their pastor so their church could evangelize the world.

God heard their prayers. Metropolitan Baptist Church became the largest in the world (over 10,000 attendees weekly) in the biggest and most influential city in the world, the capital of the British Empire.

In 1973, I (Elmer) led all 420 Liberty University students on a lecture tour of the English revival of the First Great Awakening, and we visited Spurgeon's church. Bombs in World War II had destroyed the building, but the basement was still intact. The parlor table and chairs were no longer directly under where the original pulpit had stood: They were against a wall cordoned off with ropes. Faded red pillows sat on the chair seats. At that time, the church averaged about four-hundred people in attendance. Maybe they lost their attendance and influence because they treated prayer as a display rather than the power of God.

Lakeview Wesleyan Church (attendance four to five hundred) in the small town of Marion, Indiana, also has a history of great revivals, and hosted a gigantic leadership conference for its denomination and surrounding churches. But in 2003, Pastor Duane Seitz wanted to do something dynamic in the church's prayer ministry.

The church's old prayer room was typical, with chairs, a prayer altar, tables of literature, etc. The revitalized prayer room opened in August 2003 with God leading in further restructuring of the room following a twenty-four-hour prayer vigil. As a result, the church saw a great number of conversions directly related to prayer, an anointing and weekly blessing on the pulpit ministry, and victory in spiritual warfare in a year of opposition and spiritual renewal.

LAKEVIEW'S PRAYER ROOM

God continued to challenge Lakeview's prayer life, so the church looked again at its prayer room. A Jericho prayerwalk around their facilities in the summer of 2007 preceded the most recent renovation of the prayer room, converting it into an around-the-clock prayer watch. The prayer-station format was altered to include highly interactive activities, such as an art area, candles, subdued lighting, a rocking chair, a sofa, afghans, a small library, and even a refreshment center that all contribute to the room's welcoming atmosphere.

The new room is intensely intimate, characterized by a "holy hush" when people enter. People feel the presence of God so much so that believers from other churches come there to pray. A new passion to touch God and be touched by Him penetrates the church. Pastor Seitz says, "Admittedly, it is a bold statement to say that the prayer ministry is the most important ministry of the church! I believe there is absolutely nothing more critical than intercessory prayer."

Pastor Seitz feels that only through prayer can we experience the Holy Spirit's presence and moving. "There is no weapon half so mighty as intercessors bare, not a broader field of service than the ministry of prayer."

Sandy Thomas, prayer coordinator for the church, says, "I got the vision for a prayer room at a praise gathering in 1994 when Pastor Jim Cymbala challenged the church to once again become a 'house of prayer.' In that statement I knew God was calling me to the arena of prayer."

To cover the church in twenty-four-hour prayer, people sign up for one-to-two-hour shifts. Signup sheets are on an easel next to the prayer room on Sundays for people to sign up. Prayer Captains are "on duty" for twenty-four-hour periods to fill in blank hours and to go in the Prayer Room for those who don't show up. The captains also call people a day in advance to remind them of their commitment.

DURING SERVICE

The prayer ministry at Lakeview Wesleyan focuses on praying with and over the pastor before the Sunday-morning service in the Prayer Room. Two-member teams engage in intercession during the service for God's power and touch on lives based on Matthew 18:19–20 (NKJV): "Again I say to you that if two of you agree on earth concerning anything that they ask, it will be done for them by My Father in heaven. For where two or three are gathered together in My name, I am there in the midst of them."

Before the worship service, the team arrives at the room prepared to pray. They understand their time in the Prayer Room is a sacred commitment of obedience, time, and effort and enter the room with humility, reverence, and a focused mind-set. They then read Psalms 91 and 121 and pray with and for the pastor.

Next, the team spends time at the altar in the Prayer Room, praying for the service following the scheduled order. They can use whatever prayer style they are comfortable with. Prayer themes could include prayers for empowering of musicians, the choir, soloists, or worship team; safety for all on platform; protection over all technical aspects of the service; confidence for any who gives special announcements; obedient giving during offering time; anointing of the pastor; freedom from distractions for the congregation; open hearts to receive God's message and to respond as He leads; and salvation for any in service who are lost.

The church also encourages team members to have a prayer partner praying for them when they are "on duty."

WEEKDAY INTERCESSORY PRAYER

Intercessors are encouraged to pray an hour a week, following Ephesians 6:18: "Pray in the Spirit on all occasions with all kinds of prayers and requests. With this in mind, be alert and always keep on praying for all the saints."

Upon entering the church, pray-ers sign in with the receptionist and pick up an ID badge. In the Prayer Room they can go to any of the six specific prayer stations but usually start with the confessional station in the middle of the room to settle their spirits into an attitude of prayer. Each station is equipped with a notebook containing Scriptures related to that station's focus, with suggested biblical prayer themes. The notebooks also contain space for intercessors to record prayer-requests and answers related to the station's prayer focus. People usually spend ten minutes at each station.

Suggested prayer prompts for intercessors include asking God to reveal anything that would hinder prayer, agreeing with God that they want to be a clean vessel, and requesting that the Lord direct the prayertime and keep them aware of His presence. To strengthen pray-ers, the church reminds them in written instructions that Jesus is their prayer partner in the room and tells them to claim God's promise of Jeremiah 33:3: "Call to me and I will answer you and tell you great and unsearchable things you do not know."

PRAYER STATIONS

The well-developed prayer stations in Lakeview Wesleyan Church's Prayer Room can be duplicated in any church.

First Station: Grace

In the center of the room is a three-foot-long table covered with black cloth. On it is a lamp, a Bible, an instruction sheet, and a framed picture of Christ holding up a repentant man. Next to it is a rocking chair with a crimson afghan. Intercessors are to come to this station first to confess any sins and listen to the Lord. The remaining five stations are around the periphery of the room, each one with a small three-foot-long table covered with a floor-length black cloth and an instruction sheet.

Second Station: Soaking Chair

At this station, intercessors are to write a prayer to God for themselves, for someone else, or for a specific situation. They then attach the prayer to the bulletin board in this area. At this station, in addition to the table, is an upholstered high-back chair with a heated cushion, a lamp, a Bible, instructions, pens and paper, and more. To create an inviting atmosphere, this station has a tri-fold room divider screen behind a chair that is backlit with a gooseneck lamp with a gold bulb. In addition to various framed artwork, the station also has a CD player on a small stool with a case of worship CDs.

Third Station: Art

At this station, pray-ers can get creative in talking with God. A small floor easel with a large sketchpad on it is available as well as markers for people to draw their prayers. For inspiration, the church provides a basket on the floor with art supplies, a Bible, and a hymnal.

Fourth Station: Wailing Wall

The fourth station focuses on salvation. The area has a "homey" look with a couch, end tables with lamps, an afghan, an area rug, electric wall sconces, and artwork. It is located on one side of the room against a wall that has been covered with a brick-like wall covering. A small basket on the floor contains prayer cards, pens, tape, a journal, and a notebook with prayer-requests from each pastor. People write prayer-requests on cards, then tape them to the wall for others to pray over; the cards remain on the wall for three months. Another basket has cards that record answered prayers. A small library of devotional books also is available for pray-ers to read over.

Fifth Station: World

Opposite the fourth station is a sofa table that serves as an altar with a kneeler in front of it. At this station intercessors are to pray for community and world issues. On the wall above the table is a world map that has been cut up into pieces to represent a world torn apart. A clipboard with articles about current events is available to review, as well as sticky flags to put on the map. Scripture verses, pictures of mission issues, a map of the city, and a list of missionaries are posted above the altar.

Sixth Station: Refreshment

Intercessors can go to the three-tiered table inside the door, which has a Hot Pot to heat water for coffee, tea, or hot chocolate; single-serve drink packets; and cups, spoons, sugar, creamer, paper towels, and bottled water. Near the table is a wipe-off board with names of the twenty-four-hour captains and their phone numbers.

WHAT ABOUT YOUR PRAYER ROOM?

Not many churches have an effective prayer room where members can visit frequently to touch God in prayer. Since prayer is the vital link with God and the way to revitalize a person's life, why is a prayer room sometimes ignored?

Occasionally a prayer room is out-of-the-way, perhaps in an old Sunday school classroom that was abandoned because it was dark or oddly shaped or hard to get to. Sometimes a prayer room is filled with junk furniture from the attic of the faithful; at other times it is cluttered with out-of-date church literature. Sometimes the prayer room is inappropriately too little, too big, or too noisy. But the real reason why churches ignore the prayer room is because the pastor and local body don't feel prayer is important in the plan of God.

If your church, like Lakeview Wesleyan, wants to elevate the importance of prayer in your congregation, consider starting a prayer room.

Advantages of a prayer room

By having a prayer room, the church makes a statement to its people about the importance of prayer. It also communicates the presence of God to those who come. Having a prayer room makes possible a schedule of regular prayer at a specified place. It also promotes a community of prayer by providing a place where information can be gathered and prayed over and where answers to prayer can be posted. It also can act as a conduit between church leadership and prayer warriors.

Characteristics of a good prayer room

A prayer room can be established anywhere in a church. Most prayer rooms have a few things in common:

- Privacy. An effective prayer room can be closed off from outside distractions.
- Inviting. A prayer room should provide a comfortable place to sit, kneel, or even lay prostrate before the Lord.
- Inspirational and informative. The room should have various stations or places to prayer.
- Safe and accessible. Many churches have installed prayer rooms with an outside entrance and a combination lock.
- Organized. The room will be best used if people sign up for one hour a week. Your church could be called "a house of prayer" if every hour of the week was filled with intercessors.

Lakeview Wesleyan continues to improve its prayer room. "Our prayer room is a vehicle to promote focused, concentrated, purposeful intercession in our church body," says Prayer Coordinator Sandy Thomas. "This prayer ministry will most likely always be a 'work in progress,' but we want to learn many new ways to pray and seek God's presence."

A HEALING PRAYER MINISTRY

Christ Fellowship
Palm Gardens, Florida

Christ Fellowship[1] is one of the fastest growing congregations in America. Twenty-four years ago it was birthed out of a prayer meeting in the home of Tom and Donna Mullins. Since that day it has kept prayer at its core.

Just fifteen years ago, with only one-hundred people, the church moved from a school into a worship center that could seat four-hundred. Today, Christ Fellowship has more than 12,000 people gathering every weekend on three campuses located in Palm Beach County, Florida. The church also has a remote campus twelve miles away in a converted Target store that has more than 5,000 people gathering each weekend for worship. None of this expansion could have taken place without fervent, persistent prayer for God to use their congregation to impact the world with the love and message of Jesus Christ.

Christ Fellowship is known for powerful preaching by Dr. Mullins, dramatic worship, a multi-ministry program of evangelism and humanitarian projects, and dynamic answers to prayer. It also has a positive ministry of healing that usually occurs during and after the Wednesday-night prayer service.

MIDWEEK PRAYER

Because of their deep desire to teach the congregation how to pray, the church leadership started a traditional midweek prayer meeting. The time begins with the worship team singing two or three praise songs with an emphasis on meeting with God, which allows the people to settle and prepare their hearts. Then Pastor Mullins gives an abbreviated teaching on prayer each week, helping those in attendance to understand better the power and significance of conversing with God. He has studied the great prayers of the Bible to give insight on how people can apply prayer to their own lives. These fifteen to twenty minutes of teaching are then followed by a time of corporate, group, and individual prayer that lasts about an hour.

While the exact format varies each week, the pastor leads the congregation in various prayers of praise, thanksgiving, and petition to the Lord. Usually at some point in the service the congregation is asked to pray in groups with those seated around them. During these "prayer huddles" people share personal requests and pray for one another. They may also be asked to pray for specific needs within the church or its various ministries and outreaches. This practice helps the people to share with the pastoral staff the responsibility and burden for the prayer-requests. The leadership believes this also models for the congregation the spiritual significance of God working and moving within them as they submit themselves to prayer.

The prayer huddles are meant to be nonthreatening, so each person can simply whisper prayers with one another. The pastor instructs that no one person should dominate these groups. At the same time, if someone feels uncomfortable praying aloud, he or she is encouraged to agree quietly and pray silently.

A TIME FOR HEALING

As a part of the service, typically following the worship, teaching, and corporate prayertimes, Pastor Mullins invites individuals who need prayer for healing to come to the prayer altar at the front of the auditorium. A church elder, pastor, or a trained lay intercessor meets with each person. Most of the needs represented are for physical, emotional, or relational healing. The pastors and elders usually team up with intercessors; each person has a small vial of oil with which they anoint those who have come for prayer. Then they proceed to pray by faith for whatever healing is needed to take place in the recipient's life. The leaders do this in accordance with James 5:14–15:

> Is anyone among you sick? Let him call for the elders of the church, and let them pray over him, anointing him with oil in the name of the Lord. And the prayer of faith will save the sick, and the Lord will raise him up. And if he has committed sins, he will be forgiven. (NKJV)

James' words have been often overlooked or dismissed, but several things are clear from this passage for all believers: Prayer is necessary when sickness occurs. Since we live in a fallen world, sickness is sure to touch each of us at some point, and God's Word clearly tells us that we need to pray for His healing touch.

The passage also tells us one of the responsibilities of the church elders is to pray for the needs of the sick. The leaders of Christ Fellowship follow this assignment. Not only are they to be available to pray for the sick, but also they must believe by faith that God can heal the sick of their illness.

TAKING A BALANCED APPROACH

It is easy to see how this verse in James can be controversial or misinterpreted when viewed in light of "faith healing" ministries. Many people have taken it out of context and tied it to the "name it and claim it" doctrine. However some people have received prayer for healing and have been anointed with oil only to find their sickness did not subside. This can cause confusion and disillusionment about prayer or God and healing. Some believers who need healing have questioned whether they lack faith or if those praying for them did not have enough faith.

Christ Fellowship has taken a balanced approach to this passage. It strongly believes in the power of prayer and in the power of God to heal. The church elders anoint with oil representing the work of God in the life of the sick. Those same leaders pray in faith and stand on God's promises for the sick. At the same time they recognize that God is sovereign and has a plan for each person. Sometimes His plan and His timing are very different than ours. At Christ Fellowship the pastors, elders, and lay intercessors keep this central to their prayer ministry while holding to faith that our mighty God is more than able to heal those who are sick.

In addition, the leadership at Christ Fellowship believes that anointing with oil is a symbol representing their faith in God to heal the person for whom they are praying. It's an outward representation of the prayer of faith at work by the power of the Holy Spirit. So although anointing with oil is notably significant and practiced along with the prayer of faith, Christ Fellowship believes it is the prayer offered in faith that touches the heart of God.

James continues in verse 16 by telling his readers to "confess your trespasses to one another, and pray for one another, that you may be healed" (NKJV). Sometimes the sick person needs more than just prayer for physical healing. There are occasions when illness is a result of sin in one's life, but James does not make an inseparable link between the two.

However, due to the fact that there is a connection between confession and healing, the prayer teams at Christ Fellowship have been trained not only to pray for the physical needs of the people coming forward, but also to ask specific questions that might give them better understanding into the sick person's life. Questions regarding salvation and sin issues usually open up further opportunities for prayer and ministry. Some people come forward for an outward physical need only to find that they have a deeper spiritual need that must be addressed first.

PRAYERS FOR ONE ANOTHER

As a whole, the Christ Fellowship congregation has readily responded to this time of prayer. It allows them the opportunity to share their needs with another and seek the Lord in prayer. As a result the church is seeing people bring friends and family members who have special needs for prayer and healing in their lives. Many who attend this prayer service may never come to another service.

For many people, this prayer experience is the only place or time that they have someone who listens to their needs and where they experience true care and love. The people at Christ Fellowship know that it's a wonderful privilege to carry people's needs to God. There is an Old Testament story of the priest who carried the needs of people to God when he entered God's presence:

Whenever Aaron enters the Holy Place, he will bear the names of the sons of Israel over his heart on the breastpiece of decision as a continuing memorial before the Lord. Also put the Urim and the Thummim in the breastpiece, so they may be over Aaron's heart whenever he enters the presence of the Lord. Thus Aaron will always bear the means of making decisions for the Israelites over his heart before the Lord. (Ex. 28:29–30)

Aaron was reminded of God's heart for the people of Israel because the gems on his breastpiece represented each tribe of Israel. Every Israelite was represented in those stones, and God loved and cared for every single one. Aaron's job was to carry the people and their needs into the presence of the Lord.

In the New Testament Christ calls us "priests." And, just like Aaron, we can carry others into the presence of the Lord through prayer. As followers of Jesus Christ it is not only our privilege to pray, it's our responsibility. Ephesians 6:18 (NLT) says, "Pray at all times and on every occasion in the power of the Holy Spirit. Stay alert and be persistent in your prayers for all Christians everywhere." We are instructed to be persistent in our prayers for others. The result is that people are encouraged, God's power is unleashed, and everyone's faith is strengthened.

ANSWERED PRAYERS

Pastor Mullins teaches his congregation to take time to rejoice when God answers prayers. This process actually builds faith in others. When the church celebrates the victories, the good news will cultivate a culture of expectancy and watchfulness.

One little boy was brought forward by his parents for healing prayer. He was three years old and not growing properly nor talking. The parents reported back that within a few weeks after prayer and anointing that the boy began talking and playing. God had heard their prayers and chosen to heal this little child!

Another couple needed healing in their finances. Their business was about to go under, and everything they had worked so hard to build was crashing around them. They prayed with one of the pastors, and within just a matter of days their financial forecast began to change. New opportunities opened up and help came from the most unlikely sources; disaster was avoided. They were quick to report the financial healing that came their way as a result of prayer.

A woman sought prayer for her brother who was dying with stage-four cancer. A few ladies gathered around this woman and anointed her with oil on behalf of her brother. Together they believed God for a miracle regardless of what the doctors were saying. They knew that God was greater than any negative medical report. A few weeks passed and that same woman came back to share that her brother was getting stronger. The doctors were confused as to how someone in his condition could recover so quickly. The church rejoiced as they witnessed the power of God responding to a few seeking Him in prayer.

Too often we forget to celebrate God's answers to our prayers. Many times we seek the heart of God with a need we are facing, and when He comes through, we forget to thank Him for the deliverance. When the church reviews what God is doing among them, it builds their faith to turn to Him again with their needs. They trust Him to accomplish the seemingly impossible in their lives.

A PRAYING CHURCH

Pastor Mullins was raised in a church that prayed. In fact, he grew up in an old-fashioned Wednesday-night prayer meeting. People would gather to pray during the entire service, either in small groups throughout the sanctuary or around the altar. He describes these concerts of prayer as "experiences that drew me so close to the very presence of God, reminding me that He was closer to me than I often realize." It is this influence that shapes the foundation of prayer at the heart of Christ Fellowship's doctrine and practices.

The church has prayer teams that pray over and during each service in a prayer room with a video feed of the sanctuary. As the service progresses, the prayer team covers each element—especially the pastor—in prayer. These faithful prayer warriors understand well that what happens of any true significance happens because of prayer and the move of the Holy Spirit.

The leadership of Christ Fellowship frequently mentions the prayer team's faithfulness, and now people in the congregation drop off prayer-requests to the prayer room so that the team can pray over these needs. Pastor Mullins states, "As a pastor and one responsible to share the Word of God with our people, it is essential to my effectiveness that I know that people are praying specifically for me as I preach. I truly experience the power of our prayer team's prayer when I see lives being radically transformed for Jesus."

The elders lead the church through prayer. In fact, they refuse to vote on anything without first bathing the issue in prayer. Serious decisions on church direction and vision are met with days of prayer and fasting. Only when the elders have come to a place of complete consensus of what God is directing them to do, do they act. Through prayer God has literally guided and directed the church. As a result,

Christ Fellowship has seen God do miraculous things in the congregation. It was forty days of fasting and prayer that overcame a negative vote by local officials for the church to build a 2,500-seat auditorium.

Pastor Mullins knows the power of prayer. The church knows it's not by man's power or by the buildings and programs but by the Spirit of the living God that anything of lasting significance occurs.

CHAPTER 7

INTERCESSION FOR LEADERSHIP

*Central Christian Church of East Valley
Mesa and Gilbert, Arizona*

W e want to move from belief in prayer to practicing prayer." According to Pastor Paul Covert, this is the passion behind the well-organized and highly effective prayer ministry of Central Christian Church of East Valley, which meets on two campuses in Mesa and Gilbert, Arizona. Covert, full-time pastor of prayer, is determined to help people go beyond a basic belief in prayer by motivating the church to follow the example and vision of Jesus, who declared that His house would be a house of prayer for all nations (see Mark 11:17).

In 1959, Mesa was a growing city with a population of 30,000 when Central Christian Church held its first worship service with sixteen people in attendance. Four years later they held their first service in their own building. Under the leadership of their third pastor, Dr. LeRoy Lawson, the church relocated to 33 acres of land and completed a $4 million worship center in 1986. Additional facilities were added before Dr. Lawson left the church in 1999 to become president of Hope International University in Fullerton, California.

Cal Jernigan began his term as senior pastor on April 19, 1999. In recent years, under his leadership and with an obvious sense of God's blessing, Central closed escrow on more than 155 acres of land located 20 minutes from the Mesa campus in nearby Gilbert. The first phase of Central's Gilbert campus, consisting of 98,000 square feet and 4 buildings, opened to the public in October 2007.

THE CORE VALUE OF PRAYER

A defining moment in Central's story occurred in June 2003 when the elders and staff identified the core values that would guide their ministry into the future. After determining five important ideals, they noted that they hadn't included anything on the priority of prayer. Realizing they weren't strong in this area and knowing it must be a key to the future, they crafted this statement that appears in the description of their ministry values: "Core Value #1: As a community of believers, we seek God's guidance and direction through prayer in all that we do as a church and in all aspects of our daily lives."

Knowing they wanted prayer to translate from belief to following, they hired Paul Covert, a man who felt a strong calling to a pastoral role in prayer and who had been serving in a similar capacity in a large Phoenix-area church. Commenting on his arrival in September 2003, Pastor Covert says, "At the time, two prayer meetings were held each week, one Monday mornings and the other on Thursdays. Each had an average attendance of five to six people. There was a lot of prayer going on in people's lives, but prayer was just not organized, emphasized, or well mobilized."

He prayed about the best approach to getting as many people as possible moving in the same direction in prayer in a format that would work for them. Borrowing from a model he had discovered at his previous church, Covert launched the "Upteam," which has become a powerful force for intercession for a broad group of ministry leaders associated with the church.

CONCERTED PRAYER FOR CHURCH LEADERS

In Romans 15:30–33, the apostle Paul urged the church to agonize in prayer on his behalf, birthed from their high regard for Christ and their love for the person and work of the Holy Spirit. As a leader and missionary, Paul understood his urgent need for prayer and asked for this kind of intercession on many occasions (see 2 Cor. 1:8–11; Eph. 6:18–19; 2 Thess. 3:1). As he appealed to the Roman believers, he asked them to pray for his protection from the enemies of the gospel, the prosperity of his ministry in Jerusalem, and for God's provision of rest and joy in his own life as he traveled.

Pastor Covert also understands how vital this kind of prayer is in the life of a local church. Today, God has raised up an army of passionate intercessors at Central who find many expressions for focused prayer on behalf of spiritual leaders.

THE "UPTEAM"

Pastor Covert launched the Upteam strategy a month after his arrival on staff. His goal was to find 168 people who would pray one hour a week for current and updated needs that had been submitted by the church, missionaries, pastors, directors, and church planters. That way, every day around the clock, leaders at Central receive the provision and protection of prayer.

Initially, it took three months to fill all the slots; it remains a continual process as two or three people a month tend to drop off. Yet, the system of strategic intercession is making a huge difference in the life of the church and its leaders.

Every month, Upteam members receive an updated "book," compiled by an administrative assistant and assembled by volunteers in the prayer ministry. The book contains recently submitted information from various leaders. Every missionary, church planter, and ministry leader submits two praises, three ministry requests, and two personal requests each month. Because this kind of intercession is a real priority in the culture of Central, the expectation is firm and consistent. Missionaries who fail to submit updates risk losing support from the church. The staff is likewise expected to honor the intercessors by their faithful submissions of fresh updates.

Each submission is limited to 250 words. The 5½ inch x 8½ inch book is assembled with plastic spiral binding and mailed out regularly. Each month the Upteam book contains a new inspirational quote, the names of the elders and their wives, and the prayer-requests from all the leaders organized within ministry teams.

When the Upteam vision was launched, Senior Pastor Jernigan was the first to sign up to pray. He wanted to demonstrate his own submission to this important vision both by his weekly hours of intercession and his participation in giving requests to the team. He still serves today, enjoying the blessing of praying and being prayed for.

Pastor Covert notes that people either love or hate this systematic approach of prayer over the lists of requests. "When someone drops off and we have a vacancy, we will announce it in the worship folder. Most importantly we will pray, and the Lord always sends the right people to fill open slots," he explains. Many times, he says, people have volunteered by asking for the "worst" slot of the week. He comments, "That is a real answer to prayer."

Now the new Gilbert campus has its own Upteam ministry. "It's a great way to keep a church informed on the needs of each ministry and the people who lead them. We know it's making a big difference in all we do," Pastor Covert says.

SERVICE INTERCESSION

Recognizing that spiritual battles focus on the Sunday activities of the church, Central also has a strong prayer ministry during the eight services held every weekend. The leaders consider this a hidden power source in the ministry of the leadership and the church.

Each intercessory prayer group is organized around a key prayer theme. As the services begin, the team starts with confession, then praise. Then they spend substantive time praying for the services, focusing on a wide range of issues including the pastor's sermon, the hearts of the listeners, the safety of the children, and the effectiveness of the youth programs.

FOCUSED PRAYER FOR LEADERS

Another aspect of strategic intercession for church leadership is expressed consistently as the Prayer Ministries Leadership Team meets with Senior Pastor Jernigan. He welcomes this team into his confidence as he shares some deeper and more strategic ministry concerns. They meet as regularly as necessary to hear his heart and to focus their prayers on issues that have significant impact on the congregation's health and growth.

Each week, an all-church "LIFT" prayer gathering is hosted at each campus. The format features a worship-based approach, which often flows into seasons of focused intercession for the ministry and its leaders. Once a quarter, a special all-church edition of LIFT is sponsored where both campus groups come together. At this prayer meeting, the pastor and other leaders share leadership updates and key vision points for the future of the ministry. Often, targeted prayers for the community are emphasized, and special focus is given to prayer for the leaders of the church.

Knowing that unity and mutual support among the leadership team is vital to church health, the prayer ministry sponsors a monthly staff lunch. After the meal, staff members share personal prayer-requests. Before the end of the meeting, staffers are paired up for more focused prayer. These pairs become prayer partners for the entire month with a commitment to pray consistently for one another.

Strategic intercession for ministry leaders also takes on an international dimension when the church sponsors prayer journeys in other countries. After a significant amount of training, these teams travel to foreign soil with the specific goal of prayer for nations, cities, communities, and ministry leaders in each venue.

Another recognition of the need for prayer during weekend services involves a team of prayer warriors who prayerwalk the church campus prior to the Sunday services. Once again, they focus their prayers on ministry leaders, the sermon, spiritual protection, and fruitfulness in ministry.

THE TOTAL SPECTRUM OF PRAYER

While Central's focus on prayer for leadership is one of its strengths, it maintains a broad and balanced prayer ministry that fuels the intercessory focus. In addition to having a prayer partners team available to pray with church members after services and providing both a prayer newsletter and a prayer of the month to the congregation, the church has many other areas of active prayer involvement.

Web prayer team

Central's Web prayer peam is an Internet-based program so individuals and groups can pray anywhere in the world from any computer. Participants log on to find the needs of the congregation divided into fifteen categories: health, travel, global outreach, hospital, family issues, etc. Some technical experts at Central designed and wrote the program.

For example, if someone wants to have a prayer session focused on the family needs of the church, the system has safeguards so someone can't enter inappropriate information on the Web site. Yet an intercessor can send notes to people in the church who have prayers submitted so they can tell they are being prayed for. Each request stays on the system for two weeks with a computer-generated request for updates at the end of a week. Pastor Covert notes this high-tech, user-friendly system allows the level of participation in prayer to go far beyond the old-fashioned restrictions of written communication and having to be on location to pray.

24/10 prayer

Each year Central conducts a "24/10" churchwide prayer emphasis. Half-hour slots are filled by church members via advance sign-ups. The church is able to staff intercession around the clock for ten days. During the ten days, the church provides an area where individuals and groups come to campus to intercede through a variety of interactive prayer stations designed to help participants pray about personal needs and to stimulate creative intercession for individuals, families, church ministries, and global outreach.

Different stations have been used with success. One year a station featured a large fishing net suspended overhead. Participants were asked to write the name of an unsaved friend on a paper shaped like a fish. These colorful paper fish were hung on the net with Christmas ornament hooks. By the end of ten days, the net was full and served as a great reminder of the importance of intercession for the lost.

Prayer garden

Central also has an outdoor prayer garden, since the weather in Arizona is conducive to outdoor activities. The garden provides changing devotional themes each month and offers six different prayer stations. Individuals and groups are able to enjoy a quiet devotional experience in a serene environment. The garden is open to the public.

Ironman

The men's ministry is called "Ironman." Both campuses sponsor a large weekly breakfast and study involving hundreds of men. Yet, a primary focus of the gatherings is an extended time of prayer for one another as men face the challenges of family, business, and daily life.

Annual prayer conference

Central hosts a large regional annual prayer conference. According to Pastor Covert, this keeps the priority of prayer visible, offers powerful motivation, and is vital to training more equipped prayer leaders and intercessors. Hundreds from Central attend this conference and many more participate from around the region. This event has been catalytic in fueling the ongoing vision for prayer. The senior pastor, staff, and elders enthusiastically participate for their own enrichment and as an exhibition of their support for the value of prayer.

Half-day of prayer

One Saturday a month the church sponsors a half-day of prayer that typically lasts more than three hours. They don't hold it during the summer months but consistently provide this opportunity the rest of the year. The morning includes rich worship, solid leadership from Pastor Covert and other members of the prayer leadership team, and a variety of prayer expressions.

School of prayer

A school of prayer is sponsored quarterly to train people how to pray. Classes typically run from 4:00–8:00 p.m. on Sunday nights with three topics taught, followed by time to practice each skill learned. The church provides a meal. This school is proving to be another vital equipping element to raise the level and quality of prayer throughout the church.

Special groups

Specialized prayer groups also meet, including one that prays for the persecuted church. They use a variety of tools that are available in print and online, standing in the gap for the often-forgotten saints around the world who are paying the ultimate price for their faith.

Community leadership

Finally, Central is a leader for important prayer events such as the National Day of Prayer, the Global Day of Prayer, and many other community prayer initiatives. Pastor Covert and the leadership team believe it's important to model cooperation and support for these broader initiatives.

AN AUTHENTIC COMMITMENT

Many churches spend significant effort in fine-tuning mission statements and descriptions of ministry values. Dynamic churches spend more effort in making those ideals a reality in the culture of the church. One key in the blessing of God on Central Christian Church of East Valley is leadership's resolute commitment to live their values in everyday life.

Little did the elders realize on that day in June 2003, when the Spirit prompted them to include "prayer" as a core value, that so very much would occur. Yet, as Pastor Covert notes, "They were willing to pay the price to put their money where their mouth was." The church leaders, starting with a committed senior pastor, hired capable staff, provided visible support, gave latitude for creativity, and offered consistent opportunities to the congregation in the area of prayer. Central has never been the same, and the community and people all around the globe have reaped powerful benefits.

CHAPTER 8

EVANGELISTIC PRAYER

Vietnamese Baptist Church
Houston, Texas

As a child growing up on the Mekong Delta of Vietnam, Khanh Quoc Huynh had no interest in the Christian faith. Even though he was raised in a Christian home, he was plagued with deep skepticism. Because the faith he observed didn't really exhibit God's power, it was uninteresting to him. Instead, his energies were largely consumed with fears over the threat of communism from the north.

He came to the United States, and for the last twenty-five years has been the pastor of Vietnamese Baptist Church, a praying congregation in the Houston area that is making a profound difference in the Vietnamese community through prayer-energized outreach. It is a long way from Vietnam and far beyond what he would have ever expected as a young man filled with cynicism and doubt.

Huynh's journey toward a personal faith, Christian service, and life in the United States began in 1979 when he escaped from Vietnam on a crowded boat filled with South Vietnamese fleeing for their lives. During those early days adrift on the South China Sea, facing the fragility of life, he opened his heart to Christ.

Days into the journey, the boat ran short on supplies and fresh water. People were dying. Huynh prayed, *Lord, if You will spare my life, I will give You the rest of my days in service of Your cause.* Two hours later, it began to rain providing the water necessary to sustain his life. Eventually they landed in Indonesia where Huynh stayed at a refugee camp for the next few years. In the months to follow, Huynh was feeling a great burden to preach.

A VISION FOR REVIVAL

While in Indonesia, Huynh encountered Indonesian believers who had come to help in the camp. These Christians spoke enthusiastically of the great Timor revival that resulted in many salvations and extraordinary advances in missions. It was also marked by many miracles (some controversial) that evoked great interest in the work of the Holy Spirit from around the globe. Huynh heard many stories of God at work in powerful demonstrations, further stimulating his interest in something more than the religious forms he was accustomed to as a child.

Huynh explains, "Those stories resonated in my heart. I knew this is what I wanted for my life and ministry. I longed for the clear evidence that God was at work."

In 1982, he came to the United States to study. While a student at East Texas Baptist University, Huynh's burden for revival continued to grow. He went to the school library to find books on the subject, but could locate only one. This particular volume specifically taught on the subjects of fasting and prayer. Again, it seemed the Lord was cultivating a growing desperation in his heart for something more.

In 1983, leaders from a large Baptist church in Houston visited his campus looking for someone to help them plant a Vietnamese daughter church in their area. They were willing to help the recruits finish their schooling at Houston Baptist University. Huynh felt the desire to respond to the call. In June 1983, he moved to Houston and started the Vietnamese Baptist Church. He has been there ever since.

The church was successfully established and grew steadily. Huynh was busy with all of the duties of pastoral ministry but felt a growing dissatisfaction in his heart with "ministry as usual."

BACK TO PASSION AND PRAYER

Then, at the church's outdoor sunrise service in 1989, the Lord spoke to the young pastor's heart. As he partook in communion with the people that morning, he felt a very strong impression that God would want him to get back to his passion for revival and specifically to start a prayer meeting with a focus of meeting God and enjoying His presence.

Immediately, Huynh led the church to begin a Tuesday-night churchwide prayertime. Since 1989, the church has only missed two Tuesdays and only because of weather. They are resolute in every season and circumstance to seek the Lord for His reviving power and grace. "Every week we 'go after God' for revival. We cry out for Him to change our hearts, asking that He will let us live with the same faith as in the book of Acts," he says.

In 1996, as they continued to pray, something unexplained occurred. Physical healings began to take place. "We have seen powerful visitations of the Holy Spirit resulting in salvations, restored lives, physical healings, and a greater passion for His purposes," the pastor explains.

Vietnamese Baptist Church is affiliated with the Southern Baptists who historically defined revival in a traditional sense, such as a week of evangelistic meetings. Huynh explains that he began by focusing on revival in terms of a powerful, supernatural restoration and renewal of God's people resulting in a fire to reach out to the lost in every aspect of the believer's lifestyle. This increasingly became the focus of the Tuesday-night prayertime.

A BURDEN FOR GREATER OUTREACH

With this growing burden for revival, the church sponsored two weeks of intense prayer and repentance in 1999. The pastor states, "The Lord showed up in a powerful way. The Holy Spirit moved among and within us as our prayers began to focus more on the ways we could minister to the unsaved by serving their real needs." The church felt the Lord clearly prompting them to take these works of His grace and power beyond the church walls and into the community.

Soon, church members began to minister in a nearby mall every Saturday. They set up a table, offering to pray for people about physical, emotional, and spiritual needs, with a strong emphasis on God's healing power. At the same time, they shared the gospel in personal witnessing and by handing out pamphlets.

For more than fifteen years the church has continued to conduct this ministry. On average, about fifty-five people make a personal profession of Christ as Lord and Savior of their lives each week. In recent years, the Union Baptist Association (Southern Baptist) has been inviting others from many different churches to intercede and observe this amazing evangelistic ministry.

MORE TRAINING

Of course, this kind of effort requires ongoing training. Pastor Huynh utilizes the principles of Evangelism Explosion to equip the people of the church for effective witnessing. He teaches them the concept of power and presence evangelism. "I train them to ask the Lord for insight in ministering to people. Our desire is that lost people will experience God and open their hearts to the gospel." Huynh also trains on "praying for healing, emphasizing the teaching on the kingdom of God and Christ's power over the darkness of this world."

"We have studied the approach of Jesus and the apostle Paul in the New Testament, making them our models for this outreach," Huynh explains. He has observed that people in the New Testament constantly followed these models — meeting needs, speaking to the situations of the people, and working in the in the power of the Holy Spirit in connection with their prayers. They weren't stuck inside religious buildings but were out among people, engaging in prayer-fuelled service and preaching.

Huynh comments openly about the reserved nature of his culture. Yet, because of the empowerment they have experienced in prayer and the excitement of frontline ministry to people, they have become bold ambassadors for Christ. "We now are confronting the many idols and religions of the Asian cultures with compassion, clarity, and conviction," he says. "We proclaim the saving power of Christ and then claim His authority to pray for their needs and difficult circumstances. We have seen many miracles."

OUTREACH AROUND THE WORLD

The pastor notes that even though the gospel came late to the Vietnamese people, the Lord is using the Vietnamese to witness throughout the world. He states that there are more than 180,000 Vietnamese in Malaysia and Russia. Pastor Huynh's church supports many of the Vietnamese missionaries who are serving in many of these places. He notes, "Many of these church leaders are young people who write to us and consider us their mother church even though we have never met them and cannot support them. They have studied the model of our congregational outreach and are seeking to minister in a similar capacity in the nations where they serve."

Many of those whose families were displaced by the Communist oppression are now going back to Vietnam. "They are using the training materials we have provided as they return to their homeland. Many are even going into North Vietnam. We have heard hundreds of stories from them about all the Lord is doing in and through them to minister to others in the power of Christ," Pastor Huynh comments.

Thanks to technology, the Tuesday-evening prayer meeting is broadcast over the Internet. As a result, church members are able to stay in touch with the heart of the church even if they are unable to attend the service. Just as important, believers all around the world are made aware of this outwardly focused prayer effort. Pastor Huynh has been amazed at the number of Vietnamese believers who write to him from around the globe. Many are adopting this prayer model as an important component of their Christian life and congregational focus.

A LIFESTYLE OF COMPASSIONATE OUTREACH

Beyond the weekend ministry in the mall, the people of Vietnamese Baptist Church are trained to witness, using the model of Luke 10:1–2 (NKJV):

> After these things the Lord appointed seventy others also, and sent them two by two before His face into every city and place where He Himself was about to go. Then He said

to them, "The harvest truly is great, but the laborers are few; therefore pray the Lord of the harvest to send out laborers into His harvest."

According to this pattern, Pastor Huynh trains the people to remain in constant prayer for opportunities to go into the harvest throughout the Houston area. He encourages them to stay focused and unencumbered in their approach to life. "I teach them to bless others with peace, get to know them, find out their needs, pray for them, and call them into the kingdom of God through the gospel," he says. "We have watched the Lord deliver people from the kingdom of darkness through the power of the gospel and even work powerfully to touch their bodies as He saves their souls."

The church has also produced numerous videos telling the story of what God has done in individual lives. Church members are trained to show these videos, and then to start a conversation with friends, neighbors, associates, and relatives on the relevance of these testimonies and the power of the gospel to transform lives.

STRUGGLES AND SUCCESSES

This aggressive evangelistic focus in prayer has not been without struggles. The pastor notes, "People are loyal to their traditions. Like my family, many come from a Christian culture that is rich with truth and tradition, but they aren't accustomed to living with a passion for power that leads to the presence of God." He says there is great resistance at times in getting people to pray in an outward-focused way. "In the minds of many, their faith is so weak, and they feel that they lack so much, that they do not have a vision to give their faith away."

Still, about 60 percent of the Sunday-morning attendance is actively involved in the Tuesday-evening prayer service. Pastor Huynh estimates that 15 percent participate consistently in Saturday evangelism in the mall. He also believes that the vast majority of believers in his church have a strong lifestyle of witnessing.

FUELING THE VISION

The church is able to track the involvement through the weekly reports of witnessing and ministry results. Through a variety of mechanisms, people in the church are strongly encouraged to share the process and results of their ministry opportunities. These praise statements are shared with the church so that all may rejoice and continue to pray for the work of God. Also, their vision is encouraged through the obedience of others.

Every Tuesday night at the weekly prayer service, these testimonies are shared with the church, resulting in great rejoicing and more prayer. The vision and faith of the congregation is regularly bolstered through ongoing reports of answers to prayer. Every Sunday morning, one of the leaders also gives the report of the previous day at the mall. These stories keep the vision for evangelism at a high priority in the life of the church and provide constant encouragement for an outreach-oriented prayer focus.

Another way of fueling the vision, both for congregants and leaders from around the nation, is Vietnamese Baptist Church's annual revival conference. The conference — typically held in October — lasts four days. Pastors and their wives come from across the nation to receive encouragement in spiritual revival and training in taking the work of the gospel to the streets. The work of God at this Houston-area church has been so notable that the conference is growing and serving as a tool for greater outreach in cities across America and the world, as an expression of the powerful prayer life of a local church. For more information on the conference, go to www.vbcweb.org.

THE PRAYER OF FAITH

Thomas Road Baptist Church
Lynchburg, Virginia

Two men ran across Thomas Road as big drops of rain splashed on the street. The fast-moving black cloud warned a downpour was coming. They jumped in the pickup truck as the bottom dropped out of the sky. Pop Johnson turned on the windshield wipers so he and his companion could see the building they were going to pray about.

Jerry Falwell, a young pastor searching for a location for a new church, viewed the old, bankrupt Donald Duck bottling plant through the swipes of the windshield wipers. It was not the building he wanted. Weeds grew high to cover the boarded-up windows. It was an abandoned commercial building that might hold 150 folding chairs for a church. He wondered how he could touch the world through such a building. Disappointment showed in his eyes.

"We've got to start somewhere," Pop said. "Maybe this is the place God wants us to start."

An old mud-covered rusty pickup truck sitting in the rain doesn't sound like a place for prayer that might change the world, but that's what Pop Johnson, the deacon, and Jerry Falwell did.

"God, we want to plant a church to reach the entire city of Lynchburg . . . we want to touch the world." Jerry Falwell's prayer was interrupted by the squeak of windshield wipers on the now-dry glass. "Lord, it's not much of a building. I thought we might have a much larger and more beautiful sanctuary. But we'll make it famous for the gospel, and it'll be beautiful to sinners coming to know Christ."

On the previous Sunday, thirty-five adults and their children had met for the first service of the new church without a name in Mountain View Elementary School in Fairview Heights where Jerry Falwell had gone to first grade. He had preached on the Great Commission and promised, "We will reach the lost people of Lynchburg with the gospel." Three days later he and Pop visited the bankrupt bottling plant. They prayed for God's guidance in making their first purchase for a new church. And its location — Thomas Road — would become its name.

THE FIRST SUNDAY

The first couple to arrive on Sunday at the first service at Thomas Road was Lawson "Pop" Johnson and his wife, Bertha. From the beginning they were tall, strong prayer pillars that God used to help hold up the little church.

"Hey, Jerry," Pop Johnson yelled from the open window of his pickup. "This is the greatest day of our lives."

Dust flew from the tall weeds as Pop and Bertha drove onto the empty field next to the church building. Pop helped Bertha out, then slowly reached behind the seat for the large, heavily marked Bible that he would use to teach the adult class. Bertha waved to Jerry as they started toward the church building. They were pioneers, and though they were older, they were as excited about this church as a young couple starting out a new life venture. Pop and Bertha Johnson and Jerry Falwell grinned broadly as they walked across the threshold into the combination classroom-sanctuary.

The place was just a makeshift auditorium. The smell of Lysol and Clorox was heavy in the air, because the floor and walls had been thoroughly scrubbed just the day before. Yet, their shoes still stuck to the Donald Duck Cola that was embedded in the concrete floors.

Jerry Falwell later said he might not have been able to pull off that opening Sunday at Thomas Road Baptist Church without Pop. He might have built a great church without Pop's prayer and faith, but he praised God that he had someone with rock-like faith standing with him. Doesn't every pastor need prayer support like this to help him?

The Sunday sun was shining through the cracked windows, yet the metal folding chairs were cold. In a humble way, that day launched one of the most influential Baptist churches in the country. All those who lived to see it happen knew prayer made it possible.

INTERCESSORS IN THE COMPRESSOR ROOM

One of the most sanctified places for prayer in that young church was the old compressor room out back. Brother Worley, another lay prayer giant, gathered a group of men for prayer every Sunday evening before the service. The group included Pop Johnson, Sam Pate, Percy Hall, and others. Jerry Falwell usually wasn't there because he was downtown with the local ABC affiliate beginning a televised program that would eventually reach around the world. (Thomas Road Baptist Church was one of the first churches in America to broadcast on television.)

In the early days, the room had no floor, only dirt. The men dragged in a sheet of plywood and a couple of used carpets. They knew it wasn't the place where you pray that gets results; God always looks on the heart, and He honors the deepest yearning of people of faith. More than anything else, those men yearned for God to touch Lynchburg through their church and eventually touch the world.

They weren't theologically educated or ordained in ministry. They hadn't risen to the heights of the business world. They were simple men who worked average jobs—and were prayer giants. They believed God would move through their new church. They and their wives were faithful prayer warriors whose petitions fueled the tremendous growth of Thomas Road Baptist Church.

People began getting saved in house-to-house evangelism. The TV and radio ministry attracted unsaved people to the church. The altars filled each service with people accepting Christ. The church had 857 in attendance on its first anniversary and had doubled the size of its auditorium. By the second anniversary, the auditorium and attendance had doubled again.

Thomas Road was in a constant state of revival because of the prayers of intercessors. Approximately 150 men and women pray-ers expected constant revival because God had promised, "I will pour out My Spirit upon all flesh" (Acts 2:17 NKJV). God poured out His Spirit in revival on this new church Sunday by Sunday; the Holy Spirit worked in the hearts of believers and their friends.

SAY-IT FAITH

Jerry Falwell developed a strategy for praying that worked for him. He told his small congregation their next goal, and the intercessors prayed for it. For example, he asked them to pray for a new building, additional land, a large attendance goal on Homecoming Sunday, or great soul-winning results at the altar. As God answered these goals, Jerry Falwell developed more faith to pray for bigger goals.

He based his prayers on two verses. First, to achieve big things he quoted Mark 11:23–24 (NKJV): "For assuredly, I say to you, whoever says to this mountain, 'Be removed and be cast into the sea,' and does not doubt in his heart, but believes that those things he says will be done, he will have whatever he says. Therefore I say to you, whatever things you ask when you pray, believe that you receive them, and you will have them." Jerry Falwell would note that Jesus challenged us three times in this verse to "say" by faith what you wanted from God.

Jerry Falwell developed say-it faith for effective praying. He said to his people what his request was, then pastor and people said it to God. Thus, he strengthened the people's faith and as they prayed.

The second verse was Hebrews 11:6 (NKJV): "But without faith *it is* impossible to please *Him,* for he who comes to God must believe that He is, and *that* He is a rewarder of those who diligently seek Him" (emphasis added). Jerry Falwell believed God heard his requests and believed God would answer them.

In January 1978, he walked onto the chapel platform of Liberty University and said, "We're cancelling our formal chapel program today. I want all of you to follow me up the hill to the seven uncompleted dorms. We'll all march around them once in faith, and then kneel in groups of seven to intercede to God for $5 million to finish them."

We sang, we marched, and we all knelt on the cold, wet earth to pray. I (Elmer) was praying next to Jerry Falwell and didn't know the TV cameras were rolling. The next Sunday on TV I heard myself praying, "Lord, I don't have faith to ask You for $5 million. That amount of money chokes me. I ask for faith to believe You for this amount of money. 'I believe, help Thou my unbelief.'"

Next Jerry Falwell prayed: "Lord, You've got a lot of money and

I need some of it. I need $5 million immediately to finish these dorms. When the money comes, Liberty will be able to house eight hundred more students. They will be missionaries, pastors, schoolteachers, and lawyers. I'm not praying for myself, I'm praying for them."

Then he put his faith on the line by telling God, "Lord, I believe You want us to do this. I'll tell the contractor to begin tomorrow, and I'll need money within two weeks to pay the first bills."

The money came in, the dorms were completed for the fall semester, and enrollment jumped eight hundred additional students. When I asked Macel, Jerry's wife, if he really believed God would send the money, she said, "There was no wavering in Jerry; he completely believed God would send in the money."

ANSWERS TO PRAYER

Jerry Falwell had been trying to move the church onto Liberty Mountain for decades. He challenged the congregation in 2000 to "Fire on the Mountain." Just as God visited Mt. Sinai with fire under the ministry of Moses, so Jerry Falwell believed God could send revival again to Liberty Mountain and Thomas Road Baptist Church that could challenge the world.

An early Sunday-morning group gathered weekly for prayer to put the church on Liberty Mountain. Perhaps one person who prayed with more faith and persistence for "Fire on the Mountain" was Harry Coric, a middle-age spice salesperson to delicatessens and small grocery stores. Week after week, he prayed, "God give us fire on the mountain."

When it seemed like no one else believed the church would move to the mountain, Harry believed it. Jerry Falwell had preached that the Shekinah glory cloud of fire on the top of Mount Sinai could come symbolically to Liberty Mountain, so Harry prayed continually, "Lord, give us fire on the mountain."

I (Elmer) heard his prayer weekly, but it was more than just hearing—I felt his sincerity and faith. When he prayed, I sensed that he honestly believed that what he was asking would happen. But I wasn't as sure; I didn't pray with the deep faith Harry had. On a road through Liberty Mountain there was a simple plywood sign announcing the site for the permanent home for the church. Not much outward progress was happening. Still weekly I heard Harry praying, "Lord, give us fire on the mountain."

In answer to prayer, God gave the ministry 5,000 acres on a mountain range of seven peaks overlooking Lynchburg. That was great, but no one expected a miracle the size of what was about to happen next at Liberty.

THE ERICSSON MIRACLE

Next to the Liberty campus was Ericsson, a large industrial facility that manufactured cell phones. The replacement cost for the mammoth Ericsson factory of 880,000 square feet and 113 acres could approach $200 million. Ericsson, a major Swedish conglomerate, made a corporate decision to quickly sell all its properties in North America. Five thousand jobs went to China.

By faith, Jerry Falwell believed God wanted him to have this property, so he prayed for God to lead him to submit the correct bid for the facilities. Many prayed and were disappointed when Ericsson turned down his original offer of $5 million. He said he wouldn't make another offer if Ericsson wouldn't open bids to an absolute auction. Thomas Road Baptist Church's bid for $10.2 million won the right to purchase the property.

Jerry Falwell had no idea what our Lord was about to do. The company's attorneys wanted to close the deal on February 14, 2003. This meant he needed to raise $10.2 million before that date. Thomas Road Baptist Church's banker agreed to loan whatever amount the church failed to raise so that the deal could close. Then the lawyers postponed the closing for one week.

The next day Jerry Falwell flew to Oklahoma City to meet with David Green, owner of the Hobby Lobby chain of retail craft stores nationwide and a Christian philanthropist who is committed to spreading the gospel of Jesus Christ worldwide. Several months earlier, Hobby Lobby had offered to donate a major property in the Greater Chicago area to Liberty University for a branch university campus. The Chicago property housed a new 300,000-square-foot building on 80 acres. But Liberty University officials decided the Illinois facility did not fit into its long-term plans. Jerry Falwell flew to Oklahoma to respectfully and politely decline the Hobby Lobby gift.

He had a three-hour, first-time-ever meeting with David Green at Hobby Lobby headquarters during which he declined the Illinois building and told Mr. Green about the Ericsson facility in Lynchburg. Green said, "Let me buy the building and donate it to Thomas Road Baptist Church ministries."

What followed was five days and nights of telephone and e-mail discussions and legal activity that resulted in Hobby Lobby closing the sale of the Ericsson property on Wednesday, February 19, with a wire of $10.55 million to Lynchburg. The gigantic Ericsson facility, including the 113 acres, miraculously and immediately became available to Thomas Road Baptist Church. The church paid a $1 lease fee for the first year. A year later the $10.55 million property was donated to them for $1.

It all happened so quickly and so unexpectedly! Jerry Falwell often said he found himself almost stunned at what a glorious and sudden thing the Lord had done. This donation placed Thomas Road Baptist Church $10.55 million ahead of where it thought it would be. Because God provided this miracle, Thomas Road entered the Ericsson facility debt-free. Permission was asked from donors who had originally helped the church financially to purchase Ericsson to allow it to use these funds to convert and renovate the facility. Unanimous permission was received.

THE CHURCH TODAY

Thomas Road Baptist Church celebrated its fiftieth anniversary on July 2, 2006, by moving seven miles away from 701 Thomas Road to a new sanctuary and abundant new classrooms for Sunday school. The old sanctuary seated 3,000 and only had 1,027 parking spaces; the new sanctuary seats 5,000 and has 5,000 parking spaces. The old sanctuary was located in the back of a subdivision reached by three residential streets; the new sanctuary is located where two major Virginia Expressways converge, one east to west, the other north to south.

Church attendance exploded from approximately 5,000 to more than 11,000 attendees at four Sunday services in three different venues. The large growth represented young families that had been the focus of Jonathan Falwell, Jerry's son. Sunday school swelled from approximately 4,000 to over 8,000 in attendance. Young adults were attracted to forty new Sunday school classes.

Jerry Falwell passed away while working in his office on May 15, 2007.

He enjoyed the new campus and facilities for almost one year. Many thought for sure the one-year attendance surge would plateau after that and begin to erode. But they were only looking at the human man who led the church; they didn't see what God was doing nor did they realize a church is built on the foundation of Jesus Christ.

After the passing of Jerry Falwell, Thomas Road Baptist Church had six great months of growth under Jonathan Falwell's pastoral leadership. Over 1,800 new people were added to the church, approximately 1,200 of those prayed to receive Christ, and over eight hundred came by baptism. I (Elmer) told Jonathan Falwell to start preaching on tithing like his father did so church income wouldn't drop off. He answered, "Our offerings have never been bigger."

Everyone in the church knows that the evangelistic revival under young Falwell is because so many people are praying. The church recently completed fifty days of continuous around-the-clock praying. A motel room overlooking the church, the city, and the Blue Ridge Mountains had been rented for this time period. Members of Thomas Road Baptist and other churches committed to pray one hour, twenty-four hours a day, for those fifty days. That, plus dozens of other prayer meetings, account for God's blessings.

THE GUIDING POWER OF PRAYER

What a church prays for guides its growth and greatly influences its destiny. From the beginning, Thomas Road Baptist Church prayed to receive property, buildings, and money to advance God's kingdom. These answers are milemarkers in the church's fifty-two-year history. That very first prayer meeting in Pop's truck for property and the influence to touch the world was reflective of how the church continued to grow. God answered prayer as He led Jerry Falwell into radio, TV, and every other type of media outreach. God answered prayer as

Jerry Falwell studied the Scriptures and popularized the principles of saturation evangelism, "using every available means, to reach every available person, at every available time."[1] God was answering prayer as Jerry Falwell entered the political battle over morality.

Great prayers are sometimes prayed by those who aren't great in the world's eyes. Harry Coric, Pop Johnson, and the original deacons were men who believed God could use them to touch the world, although they had no political or business influence. Like their pastor, these men believed God answered prayer. What they were in character, they taught young Jerry Falwell. In return, he energized their vision and faith. By learning from one another, they strengthened one another. Over $5 billion was raised for the church and Liberty University; the gospel was preached to millions, and God did exploits in answer to prayer.

MANY METHODS AND IDEAS FOR PRAYER

Any Church
Anywhere

In doing research for this book, we asked more than three-thousand churches about their prayer ministries. In the responses we received, we saw many great ideas for prayer. While we couldn't highlight each church in a separate chapter, we decided to briefly mention their techniques here. Some methods are identified with one specific church; others are not.

Remember the nature of prayer is always the same—it's relationship with the Lord. We believe you will be inspired by and can learn from these approaches.

4/4 PRAYER PATTERN

Based on the Lord's Prayer in Matthew 6:9–13 (NKJV), this pattern features a 4/4 musical conducting pattern. The first segment (upward) is a focus on reverence or worship ("Our Father who art in heaven . . . ").

The second "stroke" (downward) involves response, with an emphasis on surrender and yielding ("Thy kingdom come, thy will be done . . . "). The third segment (requests) features prayers about resources and relationships ("Give us this day our daily bread. And forgive us our trespasses . . . "). The fourth emphasis (readiness) anticipates the battles and temptations of the day ("And lead us not into temptation . . . ").

24/7 PRAYER, 365 DAYS A YEAR

On September 19, 1999, a prayer meeting began that continues to this day at the International House of Prayer in Kansas City, Missouri. Praise bands rotate every three hours and continuous prayer rises before the Lord as participants come from around the world to join in this unbroken flow of worship and intercession. Pastor Mike Bickle and his staff offer a live continuous webcast of the prayer meeting, a national conference, training classes, and a variety of other prayer rooms for specific needs. While your church may not be able to accomplish this large of a feat, conducting 24/7 prayer for a period of specified days is a powerful way to kick start a fresh prayer focus in a church. For more information, see www.ihop.org.

29:59 PRAYER GUIDE

First released by Peter Lord in 1976, this guide sold more than 600,000 copies. Recently it has been revised and re-released by Strategic Renewal (www.pray2959.com). It is designed to help individuals spend thirty minutes a day in prayer and features the 4/4 pattern of prayer along with daily sections for systematic intercession.

600 PHOTOGRAPHS

I (Elmer) have more than six-hundred pictures of members of my Sunday school class for whom I pray on a regular basis. Because I have so many, I can't get to them every day, but it's my intention to pray for every person each week. Many people in church today don't know one another by name, but when they exchange photographs by classes or individuals, they learn individuals' names quickly as they pray for them by picture. I find this is a great way to memorize the people in my class when I have over 1,400 in attendance.

Sometimes when we pray over a name on a piece of paper, it's hard to visualize and identify the person. But when we see a face, it's easier to pray for that person. Also, if you are a teacher who prays for the people in the class, encourage students to pray for you also. By exchanging photographs, you motivate reciprocal prayer throughout the entire church.

AFFINITY PRAYER CELLS

During a Wednesday-night prayer meeting (or any other church service of the week), divide the people up by affinity groups such as work, age, gender, vocations, hobbies, or any other type of common grouping. When people pray in an affinity group, they are more likely to open up and pray with more zeal.

ALL-NIGHT LOCK-DOWNS/LOCK-INS

Sometimes youth groups spend all night (usually a weekend night) in their church building; this is called a lock-down or lock-in. Activities can include prayer, Bible study, worship, and fellowship. The young people not only get to know one another better, but also get to know God and to intercede to Him.

BLESSING THE CHILDREN

The Community Presbyterian Church of Ventura, California, placed door hangers on every home in its neighborhood inviting residents to bring their children to the church to be blessed by God. During the service the pastor preached a sermon on how God could bless children. Then the pastoral staff and elders stood around the auditorium. Parents with children were then directed to go to any prayer station that they chose. The intercessors picked up the children to pray blessings for them; if the children were older, they simply laid hands on their heads as they prayed.

CARRY YOUR FRIENDS TO THE CROSS

Youth groups often pray for their unsaved friends by writing these people's names on a sticky note or a card with thumbtacks. The object is to post or pin the name of that friend on a large cross in the front of the room. They symbolically attach the name of an unsaved person to the cross (this can be a real wooden cross, a cross drawn on the wall, or even a large picture of a cross). This way young people are taught to carry their burdens and their unsaved friends to Jesus. It is there they pray for the salvation of their friends and ask Jesus to intercede with them as they pray (see Heb. 7:25).

CONCERTS OF PRAYER

Concerts of prayer were first used during the first Great Awakening of 1725 and have been used intermittently during the life of the church ever since. The concept is that God receives a concert by everyone praying aloud at the same time. During a concert of prayer, some pray very quietly, others shout their praise to God. Some lift their hands, some fold their hands, and some even clap as they pray.

CONVERSATIONAL PRAYER

Many years ago Rosalind Rinker wrote a book on conversational prayer called *Prayer: Conversing with God*. She taught that prayer didn't have to be a prepared speech or formal oration to God. Rather, prayer could be informal conversations with God, just as people have conversations with one another. When a group of people are praying together following this conversational model, no one person prays long. Rather, each person prays for one request out loud, and then allows others to pray for that request or another one. The first who prayed can return with a second request and so on. Conversational prayer is spontaneous, active, and people are praying one after another in short prayers, allowing involvement from everyone. Some youth groups call this popcorn prayer.

DAWN PRAYER MEETINGS

One feature that makes the churches in South Korea so powerful is that many of their members go to church and pray every morning on the way to work. These dawn prayer meetings usually meet from 5:00–6:00 a.m. Many of the people come and pray for one hour; others pray for only a few minutes.

When we (Daniel and Elmer) come to Liberty University for early morning classes, we often see cars surrounding the prayer chapel on campus. We know these cars belong to Korean students who pray for one hour before school.

DRIVE-BY PRAYING

Some churches recognize that larger suburban neighborhoods make it impossible to prayerwalk every street. So they've organized a plan for people to cruise their neighborhoods in cars and pray for every person in every house.

Those who participate in drive-by praying are told to go to the home, meet the people, and tell them what they're doing as they drive by. It's important when you pray for people that they know that you're praying, that they know when you pray and, that you are praying for the correct need of the people involved.

EARLY MORNING PASTORAL STAFF PRAYER

Ask members of the church staff to gather fifteen or thirty minutes before they are to report to work each morning. Have them pray together for the ministries of the church, specifically focusing on people in the church who are needy, have emergencies, or other special prayer-requests. Church leaders should set an example by praying at these specific times and places for the work of the church.

FORTY DAYS OF PRAYER

Based on Alvin VanderGriend's *Love to Pray*, churches are to give themselves over to forty days of prayer. This will help the congregation's prayer life go deeper and grow fuller by developing new intimacies with God. Visit www.40daysofprayer.net for more information.

FORTY-HOUR FAST

A forty-hour fast usually takes place from Friday night through Sunday noon when the church has a special prayer challenge. The fast is effective especially when churches are having weekend gatherings such as a missions, women's, or a youth conference. Challenge the people at your church to go without eating during this specific time for spiritual blessing on the conference and/or the church.

One of the best ways to begin this kind of fast is to celebrate the Lord's Table together. That way the last sustenance that enters the mouth is the juice of the communion cup and the bread that symbolizes the broken body of Christ. Then the people pledge themselves for a spiritual purpose and promise to not begin eating until after noon on Sunday when church is dismissed or the conference is over.

GEOGRAPHICAL PRAYER IN THE SANCTUARY

Pastor Mike Grooms of Rainbow Forest Baptist Church in Roanoke, Virginia, prayerwalks around his worship auditorium seven times early each Sunday morning asking for God's blessing on the sermon for that morning. Other prayer warriors pray from pew to pew for the people who will be sitting there during the worship service. Instead of praying for people in a general way, geographical prayers involve going and touching each pew.

After the intercessors have prayed for the entire auditorium, they pray for each choir seat and the person who will sing there. Then they pray over the orchestra/praise band. Finally they lay hands on the pulpit to pray for the anointing on the pastor as he preaches the message of the Word of God.

JOURNALING AT CHURCH

Young people can keep a prayer notebook at the youth room of their church. As part of their youth program, they write in their journal what God is doing in their life, how God is speaking to them, and what answers to prayer they have had. The purpose is to keep a running account of what God is doing. Every time a youth comes to a program or activity, he or she can retrieve the journal and enter more information in it. This journal then becomes a great motivation for more prayer.

LIGHTHOUSES OF PRAYER

These prayer groups typically meet in private homes to pray evangelistically for that neighborhood (often combined with prayerwalks). These gatherings emphasize a lifestyle of praying, caring, and sharing. For more information, go to www.missionamerica.org.

LOOKING OVER "JERUSALEM"

Jerusalem was not just the holy city in Israel, but rather a symbolic word that stood for an area over which a church was responsible to reach with the gospel. Jesus said, "But you shall receive power when the Holy Spirit has come upon you; and you shall be witnesses to Me in Jerusalem" (Acts 1:8 NKJV).

The intercessor can either go alone or take a small group to a hill where they can overlook their "Jerusalem" and pray for it. When I (Elmer) pastored Faith Bible Church in Dallas, Texas, the highest spot was the Trinity River levy. I would drive on top of the levy to see all five-hundred houses in my "Jerusalem" and to pray for my "Jerusalem."

Pastor Dick Vignuelle had previously been a savings and loan president in Birmingham, Alabama. The savings and loan building was the tallest building in Birmingham at the time. He took me to the top on a Saturday night, and we prayed over his "Jerusalem." Before he preached in his church on Sunday morning, he went there alone most Saturday nights to pray.

Another pastor from Phoenix, Arizona, took me up to South Mountain on a Saturday night before I preached at his church on Sunday morning. The mountain overlooked the Phoenix valley, and it was there that he went often to pray.

It is sometimes easier to pray more zealously for your city when you can look out and see the churches, businesses, schools, places of sin, as well as where people live.

LORD'S PRAYER STATIONS

The Lord's Prayer stations are seven prayer stations set up around a church sanctuary for people to kneel and pray one of the seven petitions of the Lord's Prayer.

When this practice began centuries ago, the words were etched on the wall along with pictures to remind those who couldn't read the petitions. It was hoped that by knowing the prayer and seeing the words on the wall, Christians would learn how to read. The seven stations were "Hallowed be Thy name" (worship), "Thy Kingdom come" (guidance), "Thy will be done" (yieldedness), "Give us this day our daily bread" (provision), "Forgive us our sins" (forgiveness), "Lead us not into temptation" (victory), and "Deliver us from the Evil One" (protection).

After people knelt and faced the wall, they began asking for better aesthetics. So kneeling altars were constructed in front of glass windows, then the picture and words of the petition were painted on the window. This is the origin of stained-glass windows in Christian churches.

MAP FOCUSING

Get a large map of your church or small group's neighborhood and post it where all pray-ers can see it. Then use pushpins to indicate where known Christians live within the neighborhood for which you are praying. It becomes very obvious that there are many gaps between the pins. When pray-ers see the spaces where unsaved people live, they will pray more effectively for the area and for unbelievers.

MAYOR'S PRAYER BREAKFAST

If your city or town doesn't have a mayor's prayer breakfast, consider approaching the mayor's office about the possibility of having a special breakfast where prayer is given for the mayor, city council, city workers, and the work of the city including firefighters, policemen, educators, and the judicial system.

The church that sponsors the prayer breakfast should be prepared to not only feed the mayor but also all of the representatives from the city who attend. During this time, a short message should be presented, but not always a sermon. This message could be from representatives from the city and/or other members of the legal community. There should be a time of prayer that is focused on the unique contribution of the city to the life of its people.

MINISTRY WALL

Have one wall in the church prayer room available for posting the names of all church ministries. That way when people come into the prayer room, they can see the various ministries listed and can pray for them. These names can be large or small decorative signs, picture posters, or simple letters giving the name of a minister.

NATIONAL FLAGS FOR PRAYER

To encourage young people to pray for missionaries, post or fly various national flags from the countries where your missionaries minister. These flags can be above the chalkboard or at other places around the room. When you pray specifically for a missionary and/or a nation, bring the flag of that nation into prominence. A child could hold the flag, or there could be a special holder in front of the room. As you pray for the missionary, the flag will cause young people to fix that nation in their minds.

OPEN ALTAR

Many churches don't end their worship service with a formal benediction to dismiss the congregation. Rather, some churches have an open altar for people to come forward for prayer. The pastor announces that the altar is open after the service for anyone who wants to pray alone or to seek prayer from a pastoral staff member.

PASTOR'S PRAYER BREAKFAST

When John Maxwell pastored Skyline Wesleyan Church, he decided to hold a pastor's prayer breakfast. He personally recruited two retired couples to prepare a Saturday-morning breakfast and a second couple to clean the room and help with logistics. Another person donated money to pay for the food. Pastor Maxwell announced that any man who wanted to be his prayer partner could attend the Saturday breakfast and pray for him. At its height more than three-hundred men assembled to learn from Pastor Maxwell about prayer and then to spend time praying for him and the programs of Skyline Wesleyan Church.

PRAYER 101

If your church has a well-rounded Sunday school curriculum (i.e., different class topics meet for every quarter), consider having an introductory class on prayer for all new people coming into the church. New people usually go through a new members' class first, which should have a brief introduction to prayer. However, once they have completed the membership class, they might want to enroll in a class specifically on prayer. This introductory class would teach all the various ways of praying as well as attitudes and discipline. The purpose of this class is to develop a stronger and deeper prayer program throughout the entire church.

PRAYER BULLETIN BOARD

Churches that don't have an official printed or online prayer-request sheet can inform everyone of prayer needs by posting requests on a simple bulletin board conveniently located. If requests are received at the church office, they can be kept on a neatly typed prayer list and updated daily. Allow individuals to attach a prayer-request card (see prayer-request cards) at any time.

PRAYER CHAT ROOM

I (Daniel) have organized and enjoyed several online prayer gatherings. Participants are given log-in information in advance with a password. A trained prayer facilitator leads the prayertime, directing participants to read particular portions of Scripture, followed by responsive worship-based prayer. The facilitator guides prayers to focus on other areas of thanksgiving, intercession, and supplication.

PRAYER COACHES

If you know of a particularly effective intercessor, recruit him or her to be a prayer coach to help train and motivate others in the church to a new level of faith and prayer. Prayer coaches should be recruited, then their names and contact information should be made available. These prayer coaches could be assigned to new intercessors or to various prayer meetings so they could be available to encourage all to prayer.

PRAYER CONFERENCE

Jefferson Baptist Church of Jefferson, Oregon, has a three-day prayer conference in January to learn more about prayer. They usually have about 150–200 people involved in this conference of which about one-third of the people are pastors. They've been doing this prayer conference for the past eleven years. Three other churches featured in this book (Central Christian, Second Baptist, and Vietnamese Baptist) also have annual prayer conferences.

PRAYER DYADS

In a large room, divide people up into groups of two, each participant partnering with either the person to the left or to the right. Before the pair begins praying, give them a minute or two to get acquainted. Then one of three things can take place:

- Each dyad is given a different prayer-request and allowed a few minutes to pray for it.
- If prayer-requests have been printed and distributed to everyone, have each dyad begin praying in sequence, each dyad beginning with a different request.
- After prayer-requests have been shared with the entire group, have each member of a dyad share one personal request with his or her partner for which the other person will pray.

PRAYER HOT SEAT

In children's classes, set a chair in the middle of the room. Have pupils who want or need prayer to come forward and sit in the prayer hot seat. Then lead all the other children in the room in special prayer for that child.

PRAYER JOURNEY

Some churches travel to foreign nations to conduct a prayerwalk for the people of that region or country. Jefferson Baptist Church of Jefferson, Oregon, reports through their prayer ministry that they have sent people to Liberia, Vietnam, Bangkok, Thailand, Latvia, and England.

PRAYER LEADERS

Appoint a prayer coordinator for each ministry or group throughout the church. This means that you might have a prayer leader for each Sunday school class, choir, ushers, kitchen staff, secretarial staff, and any other ministry or program of the church. These prayer coordinators have a two-fold responsibility. First, they are to gather prayer-requests from the people in their group and lead these people in concerted intercession for the requests they have received. Second, the prayer coordinator must channel the requests to a central office where the requests are printed and distributed to everyone.

PRAYER MAILBOX

For children and youth, place a mailbox at the front of the room and write on the side of the mailbox one of the following: Prayer Letters to God, Letters to God, or High-Priority Mail.

Supply paper and pens for everyone to write his or her request. This is technically the discipline of writing one's prayers. Historically, churches with a more liturgical worship have used written prayers very effectively. However, most congregational churches have been reluctant to write out their prayers, thinking that a written prayer stifles creativity and spontaneity. However, a few years ago *The Prayer of Jabez* by Bruce Wilkinson made the use of a written prayer both famous and effective.

Writing prayers teaches children to think through what they are requesting from God. After the prayers are written out, collect them and place them in the mailbox. Remind the children that just because they have put their requests in a mailbox doesn't mean that God will necessarily answer in the way or timetable they want.

PRAYER MOUNTAIN

In America, the goal of many churches is to build great recreational facilities; however, in South Korea, the goal of many churches is to build a Prayer Mountain. The nation of South Korea is much like West Virginia in that it is almost entirely hills and mountains. As you fly into an airport you may see white masonry buildings on the top of many mountains. These are called Prayer Mountains and belong to local churches where their people go to pray and intercede to God. Some go to their Prayer Mountain to fast for forty days. Because of the spiritual nature of these buildings, the people take great pride in constructing them, sometimes carrying the building supplies and equipment up the hills on their backs.

PRAYER OF A.C.T.S.

Draw three vertical lines on a sheet of paper, and divide it into four columns or sections. At the top of each section write one of the letters from ACTS.

- A (Adoration). Have people write down what they admire most about God, tell why they adore Him, and what they appreciate most about Him.
- C (Confession). Instruct everyone to list his or her sins generally and specifically. Ask why they thought they were sinful, then have them ask for God's forgiveness (see 1 John 1:8–10).
- T (Thanksgiving). Have people list things for which they are most thankful for in their lives. Next, ask them what they are most thankful for this week and this day.
- S (Supplication). Ask the people to list what they want to ask God for. This can be a list of things they need, people for whom they've been interceding, or actions they'd like God to do.

PRAYER: ONE HUNDRED FOR ONE

Joe Guthrie from Abba's House in Hixson, Tennessee, wrote that they have a "One Hundred to One" program for praying for their pastor. They ask one-hundred people to pray one minute each and every day for their pastor. They print up small cards to remind people to pray and try to be creative by asking their people to keep their prayer- time fresh, flexible, and led by the Holy Spirit.

PRAYER PHOTOS

On a specific Sunday, have each Sunday school teacher in your church have a photograph taken with each student in his or her class. Then have multiple copies made, and make sure that the teachers and students autograph the pictures for each other. Then tell them, "Take this picture of you and your teacher and put it on your refrigerator or someplace where you study, so you can pray for each other."

PRAYER PICNIC

Invite the church community to a picnic that is provided free by the church. At the picnic, have people divide into prayer teams to pray for the various needs of the church. During this time have various cards distributed that include prayer-requests. (Make many copies of the same request so many groups will pray for each request.) Provide drop boxes where the people can return their prayer-requests with notes of how they prayed and any special prayer promise that the group used as they prayed. These prayer picnics are not just for prayer—they also give church members an opportunity to fellowship and enjoy the outdoors. They begin with prayer, focus on prayer and Bible study, and include fellowship over a meal together.

PRAYER-PROMISE TESTIMONIES

Ask people to prepare a testimony of an answer to prayer, and tie it to a prayer promise in Scripture. Then ask them to stand, read their prayer promise, and tell how God has answered a prayer.

PRAYER-REQUEST CARDS

Many churches keep prayer-request cards in the cardholder in the pews so people can fill out requests during church service. Jerry Falwell at Thomas Road Baptist Church encouraged constant requests by everyone and instantaneous prayer when he received a request. People would fill out the card and hold it out for an usher to take immediately to Pastor Falwell who would read it to the congregation. That request was prayed for the next time there was congregational prayer, whether it was the invocation, benediction, offering, or any other occasions of prayer.

PRAYER ROCKS

The Blue Ridge Community Church of New London, Virginia, has a 24/7 prayer ministry in their prayer room where there's a large pile of rocks. Attached to each rock is the name of a lost person for whom they are interceding. Intercessors hold a rock and intercede for that person. When they go into the prayer room, most of the people lie prostrate on their faces before the Lord.

PRAYER SUMMITS

These three-day retreats feature Scripture-fed, Spirit-led prayer. There is no agenda, only basic guidelines. Trained facilitators give general direction to the prayertimes. Every participant is invited to read Scripture aloud, sing songs, and pray in the areas of focus suggested by the facilitators. Arcade Church in Sacramento, California (which is featured in this book), and Grace Church in Eden Prairie, Minnesota, have hosted several summits per year for several years with life-transforming results. For more information, visit www.prayersummits.net.

PRAYER TOWER

Construct a tall tower in your church or on your facilities where people can go to pray. Christ Fellowship Church of Palm Gardens, Florida, is building $28 million of additional facilities for classrooms, offices, and other ministry needs that will contain a prayer tower. This tower will be open to the public 24/7 so people can go and pray at any time.

PRAYER TRIADS

When groups are large, you might ask for one person to facilitate two other people to pray, giving opportunity for all three to pray. After dividing the group into trios, ask the person whose last name is closest to the beginning of the alphabet or the person living closest to the church building to lead the group. The facilitator should make sure that each person has an equal opportunity to share their prayer-requests with the other two in the group.

PRAYER VISITATION TEAMS

These teams visit the sick or shut-ins specifically to pray for and with them.

PRAYER WALKING PATH

I (Elmer) have seen at least one church that has a walking path built through its property for people to jog or walk on. Throughout the path are prayer stations to remind people to stop and pray for various needs of the church (the pastor, missionaries, outreach, the sick). Several people from the neighborhood use this prayerwalking path as an exercise path, and it has opened up opportunities to witness to them from the Word of God.

PRAYER WALL

During prayer conferences, have people post their prayer-requests on one of the walls in the church sanctuary and/or foyer. Make cards, pens, and tape available for the posting of prayer-requests. Some churches may use sticky notes. A large sign should indicate the purpose of the prayer wall, accompanied by a verse such as Jer. 33:3, "Call to me and I will answer you and tell you great and unsearchable things you do not know." Some may want to put several verses on smaller cards throughout the prayer wall so that those who come to pray may claim these prayer promises.

Teach people to go to the prayer wall and touch it as they pray for the requests. This is similar to the Wailing Wall in Jerusalem where Jews go to pray to Jehovah. The Wailing Wall is technically the foundation for the Temple Mount of the original Solomon's Temple. The Jews treat this as a sacred wall where they make intercession. While we do not treat a wall as sacred, we do think that outward actions by peoples stir them to inward faith and prayer.

PRAYERWALKING

In the early 1980s, Ed Siovoso returned to his home in Argentina after having spent almost twenty years organizing meetings with the Billy Graham Evangelistic Association throughout Central and South America. He went back to his home area of Rosario and began working with churches to organize prayer for his hometown.

Ed began organizing average people to walk around a city block two at a time and pray together for the salvation of the people on that block. After three or four months he instructed his prayer intercessors to knock on each door and tell the people that they were walking through their neighborhood and praying for the people in their house. He also instructed them to ask, "How may we pray for you?" The prayerwalkers were told to carry a notebook and write down what the people wanted in answer to prayer. Finally, Ed instructed his intercessors to tell the people in each house to let them know when God answered their prayers.

Eventually, a great revival broke out in Rosario. Today there is a church of 110,000 people. Maybe your church could organize itself to walk around every block in your neighborhood. In so doing, pray for every person in every house within your neighborhood.

P.U.P. (PRAYING FOR UNREACHED PEOPLE)

These intercessory groups meet regularly to pray for unreached people groups around the world. Using information available at different Web sites, they can pray intelligently and specifically about the needs and challenges in some of the least evangelized peoples of the world.

PURGING YOUR SINS

Pass out small sheets of paper and pens to everyone in your group and ask them to list their sins. Remind them that this is a voluntary exercise and that the paper will not be collected for anyone to see. Then give the people a moment to pray to God, confessing their sins and asking Him to forgive them. Give time for meditation and contemplation so they fully understand any alienation from God because of their sins. Also give them time to realize that their sins are forgiven by God (see 1 John 1:7).

Have a candle burning in front of the room when people are writing their sins. Collect all the papers. Then touch them with the candle and allow them to burn in a metal pan in front of everyone. Let people know their sins have been forgiven and purged by the blood of Jesus Christ. The most important thing here is inward relationship with God, as reflected by outward things such as candle, flames, and burning.

SOLEMN ASSEMBLY

A solemn assembly was identified in the Old Testament: "Blow the trumpet in Zion, sanctify a fast, call a solemn assembly" (Joel 2:15 KJV). Its purpose was to show remorse and repentance for the sin of God's people. Joel commanded, "Let the priests . . . weep . . . let them say, 'Spare Your people O LORD, and do not give Your heritage to reproach'" (2:17).

The solemn assembly I (Elmer) attended wasn't a church meeting you go to for enjoyment or motivation. It was for solemn prayer for God to forgive the sins of the nation. The service was three hours of praying, confessing our national sin of abortion, interceding to God for Him to show His mercy on our country, and to forgive our sins.

SPURGEON'S PRAYER ROOM

Charles Spurgeon had a place under his pulpit in the church basement where people gathered to pray for power as he preached. Set aside a place in your church underneath the pastor's pulpit, if possible, where members can gather to pray during the preaching services. Provide a table and chairs at the spot where they will be praying. If there are cushions on the chairs, they can be used to kneel on when people begin praying during the sermon.

UPPER ROOM

Whereas most churches call it the prayer room, Pastor John Maxwell had a room located almost above the pulpit where organ equipment once had been that he had renovated for intercession specifically during a church service. The floor, walls, and ceiling were covered with carpet, and an altar was built on three of the four walls where people could kneel and pray. Once he had organized a group of pastoral prayer partners, they prayed during the entire time when he was preaching.

GLOSSARY OF PRAYER TERMS

P rayer is always a relationship between God and His people; it's nothing more and nothing less. But the ways in which God's people express prayer are many. Sometimes it is one person praying (solo prayer); sometimes it's prayer partners (two-pray). When many pray out loud together, it's a concert of prayer; when people wait silently in God's presence, it is silent prayer.

Prayer can deal with sin (confession prayer); at other times it's rejoicing in God's goodness (praise or magnify prayer). When we want to focus on God and Him alone, it is worship prayer. When we need things, it's asking prayer, and when we call on God to save an unsaved person, it's intercession prayer. When we pray for the sick, it's faith praying because "the prayer of faith will save the sick" (James 5:15 NKJV).

When we feel lost and alone, we use the prayer of abandonment; when we've failed or made terrible mistakes, it's the prayer of brokenness. We should always remain in the spirit of prayer ("pray without ceasing" [1 Thess. 5:17 NKJV]). When we pray about the small things of our life, it's minutia praying.

Use this glossary of prayer terms to increase the ways that you pray to God.

Abandonment, Prayers of—When we don't know what we want God to do in a situation, so the outcome (and ourselves) is yielded to Him.

Agree-pray—Prayer partners coming in harmony and on the biblical standards for prayer. Jesus promises that this agreement will result in answered prayer (Matt. 18:19).

Asking Prayers—When we make a petition to God and specifically ask Him to answer our request.

Beginning Prayers—Initial prayers that we say to God when we first enter into a relationship with Him.

Bible-pray—When we quote the Bible as we pray, so that our requests are biblical.

Blind Obedience, Prayers of—When we determine to follow God regardless of whether we get answers to our prayers and no matter what the consequences.

Brokenness, Prayers of—When we are convicted of our sin and come to the end of ourselves.

Clean-pray—When we pray after confessing our sin, forsaking it and asking for forgiveness. Then we are spiritually ready to pray.

Commitment, Prayers of—When we commit ourselves unreservedly to the answers for which we are praying.

Communion-pray—See *Fellowship-pray.*

Concerts of Prayer—When everyone in the prayer meeting prays out loud at the same time, giving God a concert of worship.

Confessing-pray—When we pray after acknowledging our sins by confessing them, repenting of them, and asking God to forgive us, then we repent and determine to live above that temptation.

Confident-pray—Praying with a joyful and confident spirit, knowing that God is listening to our request.

Continual Prayers—A state in which, through our intimate relationship with God, we remain in continuous fellowship with God as we progress through our day.

Continue-pray—See *Wait-pray.*

Crucifixion, Prayers of—When we repent and put to death a sin, attitude, or practice by promising not to do it again.

Deliverance, Prayers of—Interceding for God to give us victory over sin or unwanted practices.

Desperation, Prayers of—When we need an answer immediately from God because of an emergency or life-threatening problem.

Discipline-pray—When two believers come together habitually to pray for the right thing in the right way.

Effective-pray—When we and our prayer partners meet the conditions and pray together, getting the answers we seek. (Also known as *Success-pray.*)

Evangelistic-pray—Praying for the salvation of specific individuals.

Faith, Prayers of—Praying with the firm belief that we will receive the things for which we ask. Often this confidence emerges because God has heard our prayer and gives us assurance that He will answer.

Faith-ask—See *Faith, Prayers of.*

Fasting with Prayer—A spiritual discipline (vow) of going without food and/or water for a spiritual purpose so we hunger and thirst for righteousness as we pray.

Fellowship Prayers—When we join together with others to pray in oneness of spirit (also known as *Communion-pray*).

Fellowship-pray—When we and our prayer partners join in a "oneness" of spirit to pray. (Also known as *Harmony-pray.*)

Forsaken, Prayer of the—Searching for God in prayer when we think He is not hearing our petitions.

Geographical Praying—Praying in places in which we feel the atmospheric presence of God or in which we previously received answers.

Harmony-pray—See *Fellowship-pray.*

Healing, Prayers of—Prayers of faith that raise up the sick to restore them to health.

Hunger, Prayers of—Prayers in which we eagerly seek to enjoy God's presence.

Hymn-pray—When hymns are used to express prayers.

Hypocritical Prayers—When we pray for things in order to bring glory to ourselves instead of sincerely speaking to God from our hearts.

Identificational Repentance, Prayers of—The prayers of our troubled spirits, in which we choose to deal with the unrepented transgressions of others (including the sins of past generations) and accept the consequences for those sins.

Injustice, Prayers Against—When we use prayer as a weapon to purposefully intercede against the evil we encounter in this world and to right the wrongs therein.

Insight-pray—When we gain spiritual understanding from God as we pray.

Intercede-pray—When we ask God to supply the specific needs of others.

Intercessory Prayer—When we pray for the salvation of others.

Intimate Prayers—Prayers in which we enjoy intimate fellowship with God.

Introspective Prayers—Prayers in which we search for the sin in our life.

Jesus-pray—When we agree with Jesus for a prayer-request, knowing that He is interceding for us in heaven. (Also known as *Praying with Jesus.*)

Joy-pray—When our prayer fills another with spiritual happiness.

Listen-pray—When we hear the request of the other person and agree with him or her for the answer.

Lord's Prayer—A model prayer that was given to us by Jesus in Matthew 6:9–13 and Luke 11:2–4 that contains all of the elements that are necessary for effective prayer.

Marriage Harmony-pray—When husband and wife have marital harmony that influences their joint intercession to God.

Meditative Prayers—Meditating in God's presence without making audible requests or even carrying on a conversation. (Also known as *Praying without Words.*)

Minutia Prayers—Prayers about the little details of life.

Outreach-pray—When two agree for the salvation of an unsaved person(s), and pray together for his or her conversion.

Partner-pray—See *Two-pray.*

Praise, Prayers of—When we focus on God in prayer to magnify Him for who He is and what He has done in our lives.

Prayer Excursions—When a group of people journey to a specific location that is in need of prayer.

Prayer Habits of Intercessors—The spiritual discipline of an intercessor that helps focus his or her energy and attention on prayer.

Prayer Journeys—When people walk from one destination to another while praying for the specific needs of those along their routes.

Prayer Models—The example of those who teach and motivate us to effective prayer.

Prayer Partner—One with whom we share intimate requests and times of intercession.

Prayerwalking—When individuals or groups of people come together to walk around a needy target to pray for the people who live there (i.e., praying onsite with insight).

Praying in Jesus' Name—An act by which we can enter into a relationship with Jesus Christ, take full advantage of His death on the cross as payment for our sins, and recognize Him as the Lord over our lives.

Praying in the Spirit—Allowing the Holy Spirit to make requests through our prayers to God the Father.

Praying Reservedly—Recognizing what things should not be a focus of prayer, and focusing only on those things that should be prayed for.

Praying with Jesus—See *Jesus-pray.*

Praying without Words—See *Meditative Prayers.*

Prevailing Prayers—Continually interceding in prayer until we receive an answer from God.

Redemptive Prayers—Interceding in prayer for the salvation of others.

Resting in Prayer—Passively surrendering in God's presence as we rest in the Lord.

Search-pray—When two wait before God in prayer, searching for an answer.

Silent Prayer—Praying inwardly without spoken word.

Solemn Assembly—When Christians gather to repent of sin and show remorse for sin. Time is spent in repentance and begging God's forgiveness.

Solo Prayers—Praying individually for God to meet our needs.

Spirit-pray—When the Holy Spirit "picks us up" in prayer to lift us to a higher spiritual level of intercession.

Success-pray—See *Effective-pray.*

Support-pray—When we want the answer for which we pray, but lacking sufficient faith, we can agree with our prayer partners because of their strong faith.

Transformational Prayers—When we open our hearts to God's power and allow Him to transform our lives into the likeness of Christ.

Two-pray—When two people who meet God's conditions for having their prayers answered partner in prayer and agree that God will give them an answer. (Also known as *Partner-pray*. See also *Jesus-pray* and *Spirit-pray*.)

Victory Prayers—When we claim God's triumph over any internal or external conflicts in our lives.

Vision-pray—When the vision of one prayer partner is communicated to the other so that they are both praying for the same results in a project.

Vowing in Prayer—When we make a commitment to be faithful to God no matter what comes our way.

Wait-pray—When we are praying to God but realize that the timing is wrong for an immediate answer.

Warfare-pray—When prayer partners wrestle with the enemy, i.e., Satan and his demons, against an attack or severe temptation. Struggling against evil influences through prayer so that God can bring us the victory.

Worship-pray—When our focus is to worship or magnify God in prayer.

Written Prayers—When we recite the prayers of others or write out words that God has placed on our hearts.

NOTES

Chapter 2: The Weekly Churchwide Prayer Meeting

1. Jim Cymbala, *Fresh Wind, Fresh Fire* (Grand Rapids, MI: Zondervan, 1997), 25.
2. Ibid., 72.
3. Ibid., 117.
4 William Law, *The Power of the Spirit* (Fort Washington, PA: Christian Literature Crusade, 1971), 19.
5. Cymbala, *Fresh Wind*, 53.

Chapter 6: A Healing Prayer Ministry

1. The material of this chapter was supplied by Todd Mullins, executive pastor of Christ Fellowship Church, Palm Gardens, Florida.

Chapter 9: The Prayer of Faith

1. Jerry Falwell, *Falwell: An Autobiography* (Lynchburg, VA: Liberty House, 1997), 326.

Here's a resource
to help you pray
with more
Power,
Passion,
& Purpose

Every issue of *Pray!* brings you:

- **Special Themes** that deal with specific, often groundbreaking topics of interest that will help you grow in your passion and effectiveness in prayer
- **Features** on important and intriguing aspects of prayer, both personal and corporate
- **Ideas** to stimulate creativity in your prayer life and in the prayer life of your church
- **Empowered**: a special section written by church prayer leaders, for church prayer leaders
- **Prayer News** from around the world, to get you up-to-date with what God is doing through prayer all over the globe

- **Prayer Journeys**: a guest-authored column sharing how God moved him or her closer to Jesus through prayer
- **Intercession Ignited**: providing encouragement, inspiration, and insight for people called to the ministry of intercession
- **Classics**: featuring time-tested writings about prayer from men and women of God through the centuries
- **Inspiring Art** from a publication that has been recognized nationally for its innovative approach to design
- **And much, much more!**

No Christian who wants to connect more deeply with God
should be without *Pray!*

Six issues of *Pray!* are only $21.97*

Canadian and international subscriptions are only $29.97 (Includes Canadian GST).

*plus sales tax where applicable
